Leading Virtual Project Teams

Adapting Leadership Theories and
Communications Techniques
to 21st Century Organizations

Best Practices and Advances in Program Management Series

Series Editor
Ginger Levin

Leading Virtual Project Teams

Adapting Leadership Theories and Communications Techniques to 21st Century Organizations

Margaret R. Lee

CRC Press
Taylor & Francis Group
Boca Raton London New York

CRC Press is an imprint of the
Taylor & Francis Group, an **informa** business

AN AUERBACH BOOK

CRC Press
Taylor & Francis Group
6000 Broken Sound Parkway NW, Suite 300
Boca Raton, FL 33487-2742

© 2014 by Taylor & Francis Group, LLC
CRC Press is an imprint of Taylor & Francis Group, an Informa business

No claim to original U.S. Government works

Printed on acid-free paper
Version Date: 20130711

International Standard Book Number-13: 978-1-4665-7688-9 (Hardback)

Library of Congress Cataloging-in-Publication Data

Lee, Margaret R.
  Leading virtual project teams : adapting leadership theories and communications techniques to 21st century organizations / Margaret R. Lee.
       pages cm. -- (Best practices and advances in program management series ; 5)
  Includes bibliographical references and index.
  ISBN 978-1-4665-7688-9 (hardback)
  1. Project management. 2. Virtual work teams--Management. 3. Teams in the workplace. I. Title.

HD69.P75L44 2014
658.4'092--dc23   2013026151

Visit the Taylor & Francis Web site at
http://www.taylorandfrancis.com

and the CRC Press Web site at
http://www.crcpress.com

Dedication

This work is dedicated to my husband, Paul Lee, and my children, David Lee, Kathy Strickland, and Megan Strange. Their support, love, and encouragement made it possible for me to complete my education and start over. This work is also dedicated to my colleagues, my longtime "lunch-bunch," and my friends and neighbors who continue to support and encourage me without fail. And, last but most importantly, this book is dedicated to all those individuals who lead and manage virtual project teams.

Contents

List of Figures

List of Tables

List of Case Studies

Preface

Leadership and communications are interdependent and cannot be separated. A project manager cannot lead effectively without a good understanding of leadership theory and models. That same project manager cannot lead without recognizing the importance of communications. Communications have evolved significantly since the last century. Leadership theories and models have transitioned to the 21st century. Or have they?

Have our leadership and management theories and models changed to keep up with the modern business environment? Or do we habitually continue to use and teach them as if virtual and global management does not exist in our current environment? In a 1945 speech to the combined Belgian Senate and Chamber, Winston Churchill is quoted as saying, "We are shaping the world faster than we can change ourselves, and we are applying to the present the habits of the past." Was Churchill predicting the future of project management? Have we changed how we lead projects and communicate?

Leading Virtual Project Teams addresses the challenges that today's virtual project management environment poses to traditional methods of leadership and communication. Leadership for successful virtual team management is different from traditional, collocated project team management. Being familiar with appropriate e-leadership styles for virtual project teams and the transition toward new leadership styles, communication techniques for virtual project teams, and e-leadership competencies is an important part of managing projects and human resources in successful organizations today.

By recognizing how virtual teams are different from traditional teams, those managing virtual projects may be able to offer benefits to the organization by providing positive, successful leadership and exceptional communications—resulting in better project deliverables and products. This book provides an approach that explores all facets of e-leadership—from how traditional leadership theories and models can be applied by 21st century leaders to providing methods by which the virtual project manager can enhance virtual project communications to meet the needs of our modern global business world.

Acknowledgments

I extend my unending gratitude to my colleague and friend, Dr. Ginger Levin. As a mentor, coach, advisor, and friend, she is always encouraging me to continue striving to be the best I can be. And I would be remiss not to acknowledge Annette Larsen, who truly understands my journey. I also acknowledge all the individuals who shared their stories, best practices, and lessons learned about virtual project management for this book.

About the Author

Margaret R. Lee, PhD, PMP®, has a doctorate in organization and management/project management from Capella University and is principal for LEE Consultants. Dr. Lee's consulting practice assists educational facilities in strategically planning virtual project management and e-leadership development curricula and also provides basic project management training and consultation for small businesses to international corporations. LEE Consultants is a Registered Education Provider (REP) for the Project Management Institute (PMI). Lee's professional experience includes corporate trainer, instructional designer, and project manager. She currently teaches at Blackburn College in Carlinville, Illinois, and Benedictine University in Springfield, Illinois. She also teaches online for the Florida Institute of Technology and the University of Northwestern Ohio and is a frequent guest presenter at the University of Wisconsin–Madison Fluno Center for Executive Education and for Project Management Institute chapters throughout the United States.

Dr. Lee is a referee for the *International Journal of Project Management,* is on the editorial review board for the *International Journal of Mentoring and Coaching in Education,* and was a reviewer for the 2012 PMI's Research & Education Conference. An active member of the PMI Central Illinois chapter, she is a facilitator for their Springfield, Illinois, division's PMP Exam Review Course Certification Training. Her recent presentations include "Using Discussion Forum Rubrics as a Teaching Strategy to Enhance Collaborative Learning in Online Courses" at the Association for the Advancement of Computing in Education (ACCE) World Conference on Educational Media and Technology; "Stakeholder Management" for the University of Wisconsin–Madison School of Business Fluno Center for Executive Education; and "Moving beyond the Ordinary Project Management Curriculum at the Graduate Level" as a panel symposium member at the PMI's Research and Education Conference.

Dr. Lee's articles can be found in the *Journal of Project, Program and Portfolio Management,* Special Issue: Project Management Education in the Online World; *Roadmap—Project Portfolio Management in Project Management Consulting Journeys, Destinations, and the Best Paths to Take; Training and Management Development Methods; International Journal of*

Project Management; and *International Journal of Aging and Development: A Journal of Psychosocial Gerontology.* She has published chapters in the following texts: *Project Management*; *Public Leadership* and *Encyclopedia of E-Business Development and Management in the Digital Economy, Volume II.*

The Project Management Professional® (PMP®) is a registered trademark of the Project Management Institute, Inc.

Lee can be reached at LEE Consultants
www.LEE4consulting.com

Introduction

WHAT'S IN THIS BOOK?

Leading Virtual Project Teams is divided into five chapters. It begins by looking at the factors affecting the movement from traditional work environments to virtual organizations and the challenges of leading multicultural, global organizations.

The next chapter reviews e-leadership—what it means and the application of traditional and new leadership models and theories to virtual project management. How can we begin to move toward multiple e-leadership styles and what are the benefits of doing so?

Chapter 3 covers virtual project communications and the tools and techniques to enhance communications for distributed teams. This chapter includes various approaches to communicating in a distributed work environment and best practices. Which leadership styles are best suited for good communications in the virtual environment? How can the virtual project manager improve communications for the team?

Multicultural communications are the topic for Chapter 4. By understanding cultural differences globally and within the organization, the project manager can work toward increasing efficiency and productivity by using progressive communication skills and techniques. How do the primary dimensions of culture affect our global conversations? How can the e-leader effectively integrate multiple cultures to provide the best possible culture for teams?

The final chapter of this book provides a detailed discussion of competencies for e-leaders, going beyond virtual project communications to the e-leadership skills necessary for project managers who want to further the success of the 21st century organization. A discussion of best practices concludes this chapter and includes managing and motivating the multicultural team, controlling social isolation and cyberbullying in the virtual environment, and e-ethics.

Case studies help provide real-world application to the virtual challenges presented in each chapter.

HOW CAN THIS BOOK HELP ME?

Leading Virtual Project Teams presents fresh approaches for and adapts existing leadership theories to the challenges presented by virtual project management. It provides the virtual project manager with progressive tools and techniques to improve e-leadership and communications.

For educational institutions, this book provides a text for accredited project management programs that can be used to increase the understanding and definition of project management leadership and communications outside the traditional project environment. It is useful for academic or professional classes that provide project management and leadership theory and for studying virtual, multicultural communications. For project management programs and academic audiences, the book provides references, theory analyses, and scholar–practitioner perspectives.

WHY IS THIS IMPORTANT NOW?

Successful virtual communications have become increasingly important and necessary in managing nontraditional projects. Virtual project management poses challenges to traditional methods of communication. Virtual communication and tools and techniques to enhance communication for virtual organizations have become progressively more necessary. By recognizing how virtual teams are different from traditional teams, those managing virtual projects may be able to offer benefits to the organization by providing positive, successful leadership, resulting in better project deliverables and products.

SOURCES, RESOURCES, AND INSPIRATION FOR THIS BOOK

Many individuals shared their stories, best practices, and lessons learned about virtual project management for this book through survey responses and interviews. Although they all preferred to remain anonymous, their perspectives make this book relevant and real world. Anonymous quotes from virtual project managers were taken from survey responses from the author's doctoral dissertation (2011). Anonymous interviews were conducted with virtual managers involved in all types of projects and project teams and were recorded by the author in 2013 for use in this book. Inspiration for much of this book was drawn from Parviz Rad and Ginger Levin's text *Achieving Project Management Success Using Virtual Teams* (Boca Raton, FL: J. Ross Publishing, 2003).

1

Overview

VIRTUAL TERMINOLOGY

Knowing the definitions of terms such as *projects, virtual, virtual project leadership,* and *e-leadership* is important to the basic premise of leading virtual project teams. Recently, a group was discussing virtual team leadership, and one individual asked what that meant. His understanding of the term *virtual* was "not real or existing, hypothetical, or impossible." Determining leadership of something that was not real did not match his contextual background.

It is fundamental to define and understand specific terms to begin a conversation about organizations that embrace virtual projects. "A *project* is a temporary endeavor undertaken to accomplish a unique product, service, or result" [1] with a definite beginning and end. A *successful project* is defined as a project that is implemented on time, on budget, and with the required quality level defined by the customer(s) [2]. The Project Management Institute's definition is similar and states that project success is measured by "product and project quality, timeliness, budget compliance, and degree of customer satisfaction" [3].

The *project manager* or *project leader* is responsible for leading the project team to the conclusion of the project. The project manager uses tools, skills, and techniques gained through the study of project management to successfully meet the requirements of the project and complete the project on time, in scope, within budget, and to the satisfaction of the key stakeholders and sponsors.

Ariss, Nykodym, and Cole-Laramore [4] define a *virtual team* as a group of skilled individuals who communicate electronically. *Virtual organizations* reflect the ever-evolving nontraditional work environment of the 21st century, with virtual team members collaborating from geographically distant locations [5]. These virtual teams share a common work, product, or project goal and work together—often without physical interaction [6]. Virtual organizations are proliferating in business today and will continue to become more popular in the future [7]. Even though many organizations and industries have managed projects successfully for decades using a distributed model via regional offices or the use of subcontractors, the explosion of the Internet and electronic communications has brought virtual project management and organizations to the forefront in today's business environment. Virtual organizations consist of employees who are not collocated and work from anywhere in the world, allowing the organization to operate globally and without brick-and-mortar boundaries.

Virtual teams can be further defined organizationally as *matrix, virtual reporting,* or *extended* [8] models. In a matrix team, individuals work across functional silos and have multiple reporting lines and competing goals. In virtual reporting teams, individuals may spend only a portion of their time working on the team and are members of multiple teams. In extended teams, the team may include customers, suppliers, or partners outside the organization who need to collaborate effectively. Virtual teams can also follow a *traditional virtual* model, defined by team members who are geographically dispersed doing common work with a shared product or project goals. Virtual teams can then be defined even further by type [9,10]:

- *Networked*—diverse and fluid work, with membership changing often, internal and/or external team members
- *Parallel*—short-term work, distinct membership, internal and/or external team members
- *Product*—work has a defined beginning and end date and is usually longer term, members may move on and off the project as needed by skill set but team boundaries are clear, defined membership
- *Work or production*—ongoing work done electronically, with functional, defined membership
- *Service*—continuous customer service or support work done electronically, with functional, defined membership

- *Action*—work as needed (emergency response) and usually immediate, specialized and team boundaries are unclear, fluid or defined membership
- *Offshore*—continuous customer service or support, software development, specialized, defined membership

Figure 1.1 provides a graphic illustration of the organizational models and types of virtual teams as defined above.

Virtual Organizational Model(s)	Type of Virtual Team	Virtual Membership of Team	Stability of the Virtual Team Membership
Matrix Virtual Reporting Extended	Networked—diverse and fluid work	Internal and/or external team members	Membership changes often
Matrix Virtual Reporting Extended	Parallel—short-term work	Internal and/or external team members	Distinct membership
Matrix Traditional	Product—work has a defined beginning and end date	Members may move on and off the project as needed by skill set	Defined membership
Traditional	Work or production—ongoing work done electronically	Functional areas	Defined membership
Traditional	Service—continuous customer service or support work done electronically	Functional areas	Defined membership
Virtual Reporting Extended	Action—work as needed (emergency response)	Specialized—external	Fluid or predefined membership
Virtual Reporting Extended	Offshore—continuous customer service or support, software development	Specialized—external	Defined membership

FIGURE 1.1
Chart of organizational models and types of virtual teams.

Managers can be categorized as *traditional* (not managing virtual employees), *virtual* (managing only virtual employees), or a *hybrid* (managing a combination of traditional and virtual employees). Garton and Wegryn [11] suggest that although traditional management remains the primary form of management, certain industries are seeing traditional management decline and virtual or hybrid managers becoming the norm. Traditional does not suggest old-fashioned or wrong. The 21st century traditional manager is collocated with the employees but probably uses electronic communications such as e-mail, instant messaging, cloud-based databases, and other tools to manage. In the collocated team the traditional manager often becomes the primary spokesperson for the project and is clearly in control of the project. However, many organizations recognize that some work needs to be centralized and other work can be virtual or outsourced.

Hybrid teams are prevalent in organizations and are the most common type of virtual team. Leaders of hybrid teams face the challenge of being competent at managing both traditional collocated team members and virtual, global team members—and must be able to demonstrate success with both styles of leadership. The hybrid leader is seen as the primary contact in the collocated environment but needs to recognize that in the virtual environment, leadership is typically shared among team members based upon skill or task. A completely virtual manager works entirely remotely, as do all members of the project team, using only electronic means to communicate and holding virtual team meetings. The truly virtual manager shares control and authority with the team members and leads facilitative and administrative functions as well as integrates the work, motivates, builds trust and relationships, and ensures communication among the project team members.

The term *e-leadership* refers to leadership of those projects with virtual teams or teams that are not collocated. e-Leadership is necessary in the virtual business environment where work is conducted through information technology [12] as opposed to traditional, collocated teams of workers. e-Leadership skills are important to the success of virtual project work. Virtual management and traditional management both fill the organizational needs. The need for e-leadership in virtual project teams has become increasingly relevant as businesses move toward more nontraditional work [13]. Understanding this need is primary to the success of the organization's virtual projects. The virtual environment presents unique challenges to leadership, most particularly in communications, which may impede primary leadership functions if managed incorrectly [14]. Primary leadership functions include communicating, influencing, decision making, and managing [15]. Nontraditional or virtual project teams and teams that are not collocated require project managers with virtual experience [16] and training in e-leadership [17]. Virtual managers need training for virtual skill sets, including management strategies and styles, communication techniques, and cross-cultural skills [18]. Strong leadership and management skills in the traditional environment do not necessarily transfer to the virtual environment. Often managers will continue using traditional processes in the nontraditional, virtual environment with poor-quality results and unhappy, frustrated project teams. What works in the collocated environment often just does not "go according to plan" in the virtual environment. Master of business administration (MBA) and leadership programs stress leadership theories and styles— but few explore how they are applied in the virtual environment. Existing research and how-to books on e-leadership and project success generally do not specifically address e-leadership and virtual project success to provide and promote techniques to enhance a project, and therefore, organizational success [19].

FACTORS AFFECTING THE MOVEMENT FROM TRADITIONAL WORK ENVIRONMENTS TO VIRTUAL ORGANIZATIONS

In 1995, Grove [20] suggested an "adapt or die" scenario, saying: "You have no choice but to operate in a world shaped by globalization and the information revolution." The movement from the 20th century work environment to our current, virtual and global work environment reflects this philosophy and can be studied on multiple levels. It is necessary to analyze the factors affecting the movement away from the traditional work environment into the virtual team environment to understand the challenges faced in managing virtual organizations.

Downsizing, rightsizing, outsourcing, reorganization, and *reengineering* are all terms used to describe organizational attempts to reduce the size of the workforce. Reduction strategies that are strategically planned to increase the strength of the organization reflect the current ever-changing business environment [21] and are encouraging the creation of more virtual work environments. Successful virtual project management is becoming more important and necessary in managing virtual human resources. But the statistics generated from these activities often do not account for the increase in new job creations, the development of virtual teams, or the flattening of matrix structures within organizations, termed *employment redefinition* [22]. These activities have created positions outside the traditional office and organizational structure that deviate from previously embraced 20th century concepts and enhance the organization's competitive advantage. By employing virtual workers, businesses often find that they are attracting, engaging, and retaining top talent and fulfilling new organizational resource needs.

Organizations have many other reasons to restructure in today's global and economic business climate. New emerging markets, regional regulations, operating costs, and access to knowledge bases and resources are a few of the drivers behind the emerging trend away from traditional work environments to virtual work environments [23]. Changes are being made to traditional organizations to maximize time to market, production quality, cost reduction, and competitive advantage. Global competition and the pressures of a global marketplace, technological advances, flatter organizational hierarchies, and rising customer expectations have caused restructuring and geographical distribution of many organizations' resources [24]. To compensate for these 21st century challenges, organizations are turning to virtual work and decentralized systems.

Advantages include less expense in the need to relocate employees, reduced real estate costs, increased expertise on teams, around-the-clock work because of different time zones, less expensive cross-functional interaction, improved customer service, and the elimination of travel and physical office expenses—and the list of advantages continues to grow. According to Sheridan [25], 82% of *Fortune* magazine's "100 Best Companies to Work For" embrace virtual work and support virtual work policies. As organizations realize fewer overhead costs and a reduction in carbon footprint, their virtual team members demonstrate increased productivity, better health and wellness, reduced absenteeism (a reduction of 3.7 days per year on average), higher retention rates, and reduced numbers of on-site accidents. In fact, research suggests that employing virtual workers poses less risk than having on-site workers [26]. Table 1.1 provides an overview of some of the major factors affecting the movement from traditional to virtual organizations.

TABLE 1.1

Major Factors Affecting the Movement toward Virtual Organizations

Internal Human Resource Factors	Internal Financial Factors	External Factors
Downsizing/Rightsizing	Exploding operating and overhead costs, need for cost reduction	New emerging markets
Organizational reorganization/ Reengineering	High travel and physical office expenses	Government and regional regulations
Outsourcing	Increases in production quality expenses	Time to market
Flatter organizational hierarchies	Retention savings by restructuring and geographical distribution of resources	Virtual access to knowledge bases and resources
Rising customer expectations, need to improve customer services	High employee relocation costs	Global competition/global marketplace
Technological advances	High real estate costs	Technological advances
Need for increased expertise and specific skill sets on teams	Increased costs for health and wellness, absenteeism, on-site accidents	Need to improve competitive advantage
Need for cross-functional interaction to manage efficiently	Desire to and incentives to reduce carbon footprint	Demand for around-the-clock accessibility

CHALLENGES OF LEADING IN VIRTUAL ORGANIZATIONS

Recognize, however, that with these advantages comes a list of new challenges for the leaders of virtual teams. Cascio [27] suggests that there are disadvantages to virtual work, including setup and maintenance costs and cultural issues. Included in this list are the challenges of isolation and lack of trust between team members, both of which may lead to communication issues and productivity problems.

Leading in the virtual environment poses challenges to those accustomed to traditional work groups in functional organizations. Virtual program and project management demands a new approach that requires evaluation of the advantages and disadvantages of nontraditional work and the leadership competencies to manage at a virtual level. In an organization experiencing resource restrictions and growth that involves an evolution to a cross-functional virtual environment, interpersonal skills and the ability to be an agent of change are important skills. The inability to lead through the challenges of working virtually and moving toward a new organizational structure presents a huge risk to the organization.

Research [28,29] supports the complexities of virtual management and suggests that the following are some of the challenges that contribute as social influences that make managing virtual teams difficult:

- Language barriers that reduce the opportunities for information communication
- Differences in interpreting context—such as high-context cultures (Asian, Arabian, Southern European) versus low-context cultures (Swiss, German, American, Australian)
- Differences in perception of what cannot be "seen" during virtual communications (in the virtual world, team members can only perceive what is directly in front of them)
- Differences in perceived status (manager versus team member, hierarchy within the team members)
- Cultural differences and different company cultures when using global vendors or consultants
- Time zone confusion and consideration of time zone differences in virtual communications

Coordinating team members in different time zones is the most commonly mentioned challenge for virtual team leaders by the study participants in Hambley, O'Neill, and Kline's [30] research. Communication presents itself as a recurrent thread among the challenges encountered in virtual program and project management research. Another study [31] lists challenges in managing virtual teams as intercultural and team communications, defusing conflicts and building trust, and cultural differences in work emphasis and deadline adherence. Goodbody [32] suggests team communication, trust and collaboration, and team formation as critical success factors for managing virtually. Difficulty in finding information and difficulty in integrating information created with different tools are also challenges [33]. A fundamental problem to virtual management is the failure to maintain and establish shared knowledge by team members and how that knowledge will be disseminated. Nonverbal communication is essential in interpersonal relationships, and virtual environments lack this ability to communicate, making it challenging to capture the nonverbal cues [34]. Haywood [35] suggests that virtual teams are harder to manage, citing that communication is the primary challenge, and Kliem [36] posits that many challenges hinder communication effectiveness. Among these are unidirectional communication, overemphasizing data and information, lack of understanding of the intended audience or stakeholders, not enough face-to-face interaction, relying on only one communication approach, and stressing the negative.

The inventory of challenges continues as multiple researchers and writers provide lists of the problems faced when leading project teams. Zofi [37] suggests several challenges to leading project teams. The first is the challenge of building virtual relationships and rapport with the virtual team members. The second is observing, evaluating, measuring, and assessing the work being done, along with the virtual team members' skills, development, and competencies. The list concludes with communication as a major challenge, probably the most common challenge found in reviewing virtual project team management. With more than 80% of virtual team communication being nonverbal [38] (electronic), communication becomes a major issue for successful virtual project management. Traditional project environments provide leaders the opportunity to communicate and implement projects with team members located in the same physical geographic location using face-to-face meetings as the primary method of communication [39], but virtual management poses challenges to these traditional methods of communication.

Monitoring and controlling the project is another common challenge listed—from delegating work to tracking progress and deadlines to handling conflict. The project manager faces the challenge of building a strong team within a virtual environment, and doing so with little or no power and control. In fact, *control* is an outdated management concept for virtual leadership and usually is ineffective in the virtual environment. Instead, e-leadership requires controlling processes—not people—to enable and empower virtual team members to "control" themselves. Virtual project managers face the challenge of not actually seeing or knowing what the virtual employee is doing at any one particular time, and accountability issues can arise in the bounds of the structure of the virtual project team. With virtual leadership, challenges with visibility and transparency as to what the team members are doing and when it is being done must be addressed. Maintaining respect, promoting the project vision, setting goals, and enabling team member accountability for a geographically dispersed group can become major challenges to the project manager who lacks e-leadership competencies.

The inventory of challenges continues with technological challenges, such as the expense of equipment, support, and infrastructure necessary for virtual communications and Internet and connectivity challenges. Add yet more challenges to the list—motivational issues, disengagement of the virtual employee with the business needs and quality expectations for the company's service(s) or product(s), loss or lack of understanding of the organization's larger vision and mission—and these increase the inventory of challenges even more. Figure 1.2 provides a listing of some challenges the project manager faces in leading virtual project teams.

LOOKING AHEAD: THE APPLICATION OF TRADITIONAL LEADERSHIP MODELS AND THEORIES TO VIRTUAL PROJECT MANAGEMENT

The standard measure for project success is that the project comes in on time, in scope, within budget, and with a quality deliverable. The success rate of virtual IT projects is less than 30% [40,41]. The Standish Report [42] suggests only 16.2% of IT projects are successful, projects over budget accounted for 52.7%, and canceled projects accounted for 31.1%. The challenges of managing 21st century global and virtual projects require more emphasis to be placed on tools and techniques that will improve virtual project team communication. As the 14th Dalai Lama is quoted as saying: "I always believe the rule by king or official leader is outdated. Now we must catch up with the modern world."

Chapter 2 of this book explores e-leadership—what it is and how it can be adapted to the traditional leadership model and theories. How can we move toward multiple e-leadership styles for managing virtual project teams, and what would be the benefits in the new global and virtual environment?

Communications	Cultural Teams	Interpersonal	Technological	Economical
Language barriers	Context	Trust issues	Difficulty in finding information	Setup and equipment costs
Absence of nonverbal cues	Cultural differences regarding time and deadlines	Perceptions	Different technological tools	Maintenance costs
Time zones	Differences in work/life philosophies	Status confusion	Integrating information	Difficulties in measuring, evaluating, and tracking work
Collaboration	Lack of understanding between team and stakeholders	Conflict management	Shared knowledge bases	
Unidirectional communication	Shared leadership within the team	Motivation issues and disengagement	IT support	Virtual infrastructure support within organization
Little face-to-face interaction	Respect for differences among team	Relationship building	Internet access and connectivity issues	
Lack of multiple communication approaches	Team formation	Personal development		Missed deadlines, rework

FIGURE 1.2
Challenges of leading virtual project teams.

REFERENCES

1. Project Management Institute. (2013). *A guide to the project management body of knowledge: PMBOK guide* (5th ed.) (p.5). Newton Square, PA: Project Management Institute.
2. Kendrick, T. (2006). *Results without authority: Controlling a project when the team doesn't report to you—A project manager's guide.* New York: American Management Association.
3. Project Management Institute. (2013). *A guide to the project management body of knowledge: PMBOK guide* (5th ed.). Newton Square, PA: Project Management Institute.
4. Ariss, S., Nykodym, N., & Cole-Laramore, A. A. (2002). Trust and technology in the virtual organization. *S.A.M. Advanced Management Journal, 67*(4), 22–25.
5. Lee, M. R. (2009). Effective virtual project management using multiple e-leadership styles. In *Encyclopedia of e-business development and management in the global economy.* Hershey, PA: IGI Global Publishing.
6. Carstens, D. S., Richardson, G. L., & Smith, R. B. (2013). *Project management tools & techniques.* New York: CRC Press, Taylor & Francis Group.
7. Martins, L. L., Gilson, L. L., & Maynard, M. T. (2004). Virtual teams: What do we know and where do we go from here? *Journal of Management, 30*(6), 805–835.
8. Global Integration. (2012). Virtual team leadership: Building the skills to lead virtual, remote, extended and other complex teams. Retrieved from http://www.global-integration.com/virtual-teams/leadership.
9. Zofi, Y. S. (2011). *A manager's guide to virtual teams.* New York: AMACOM.
10. Duarte, D., & Snyder, N. (1999). *Mastering virtual teams.* San Francisco: Jossey-Bass.
11. Garton, C., & Wegryn, K. (2006). *Managing without walls.* Lewisville, TX: Mc Press Online, LP.
12. Avolio, B. J., & Kahai, S. S. (2003). Adding the "E" to e-Leadership: How it may impact your leadership. *Organizational Dynamics, 31*(4), 325–415. doi:10.1016/S0090-2616(02)00133-X.
13. Cascio, W. F. (2000). Managing a virtual workplace. *The Academy of Management Executive, 14*(3), 81–90.
14. Arnold, G. E. (2008). Examining the relationship between leadership style and project success in virtual projects. *Dissertation Abstracts International, 70*(01), 150. (UMI No. 3345049).
15. Project Management Institute. (2013). *A guide to the project management body of knowledge: PMBOK guide* (5th ed.). Newton Square, PA: Project Management Institute.
16. Foti, R. (2005). The invisible manager. *PMI Leadership in Project Management Annual, 1,* 53–58. Retrieved from http://www.pmileadership-digital.com.
17. Pulley, M. L., & Sessa, V. I. (2001). e-Leadership: Tackling complex challenges. *Industrial and Commercial Training, 33*(6/7), 225–229. doi:10.1108/00197850110405379.
18. Garton, C., & Wegryn, K. (2006). *Managing without walls.* Lewisville, TX: Mc Press Online, LP.
19. Barbuto, J. E. (2005). Motivation and transactional, charismatic, and transformational leadership: A test of antecedents. *Journal of Leadership & Organizational Studies, 11*(4), 26–40. doi:10.1177/107179190501100403.
20. Grove, A. S. (1995, September 18). A high-tech CEO updates his views on managing and careers. *CNNMoney,* Cable News Network, Time Warner. Retrieved from http://Money.Cnn.Com/Magazines/Fortune/Fortune_Archive/1995/09/18/206087/Index.htm.

21. Drew, S. (1994). Downsizing to improve strategic position. *Management Decision*, 32(1), 4–11.
22. Miller, R. A. (1998). Lifesizing in an era of downsizing: An ethical quandary. *Journal of Business Ethics*, 17(15), 1693–1700.
23. Tran, V. N., & Latapie, H. M. (2006). Four strategies for team and work structuring in global organizations. *The Business Review, Cambridge*, 5(1), 105–110.
24. Roebuck, D. B., & Britt, A. C. (2002). Virtual teaming has come to stay: Guidelines and strategies for success. *Southern Business Review*, 28(1), 29–39.
25. Sheridan, K. (2012). *The virtual manager: Cutting-edge solutions for hiring, managing, motivating, and engaging mobile employees.* Pompton Plains, NJ: Career Press.
26. Sheridan, K. (2012). *The virtual manager: Cutting-edge solutions for hiring, managing, motivating, and engaging mobile employees.* Pompton Plains, NJ: Career Press.
27. Cascio, W. F. (2000). Managing a virtual workplace. *The Academy of Management Executive*, 14(3), 81–90.
28. Zofi, Y. S. (2011). *A manager's guide to virtual teams.* New York: AMACOM.
29. Barczak, G., McDonough, E., & Athanassiou, N. (2006). So you want to be a global project leader? *Research Technology Management*, 49(3), 28–36.
30. Hambley, L. A., O'Neill, T., & Kline, T. (2007). Virtual team leadership: Perspectives from the field. *International Journal of E-Collaboration*, 3(1), 40–63.
31. Zakaria, N., Amelinckx, A., & Wilemon, D. (2004). Working together apart? Building a knowledge-sharing culture for global virtual teams. *Creativity and Innovation Management*, 13(1), 15–29.
32. Goodbody, J. (2005). Critical success factors for global virtual teams. *Strategic Communication Management*, 9(2), 18–21.
33. Lu, M., Watson-Manheim, M. B., Chudaba, K. M., & Wynn, E. (2006). Virtuality and team performance: Understanding the impact of variety of practices. *Journal of Global Information Technology Management*, 9(1), 4–23.
34. Driskell, J. E., Radtke, P. H., & Salas, E. (2003). Virtual teams: Effects of technological mediation on team performance. *Group Dynamics: Theory, Research, and Practice*, 7(4), 297–323.
35. Haywood, M. (2000). Working in virtual teams: A tale of two projects and many cities. *IT Professional Magazine*, 2(2), 58–60.
36. Kliem, R. L. (2004). *Leading high performance projects.* Boca Raton, FL: J. Ross Publishing.
37. Zofi, Y. S. (2011). *A manager's guide to virtual teams.* New York: AMACOM.
38. Garton, C., & Wegryn, K. (2006). *Managing without walls.* Lewisville, TX: Mc Press Online, LP.
39. Baladi, I. (2008). An empirical analysis of perceived value of virtual versus traditional project management practice. *Dissertation Abstracts International*, 68(09), 121. (UMI No. 3277885).
40. Goodbody, J. (2005). Critical success factors for global virtual teams. *Strategic Communication Management*, 9(2), 18–21.
41. King, J. (2003, June 23). Survey shows common IT woes. *Computerworld*. Retrieved from http://www.computerworld.com/s/article/82404/Survey_shows_common_IT_woes_persist?taxonomyId=014
42. Standish Group. (1995). *The Standish Group report: Chaos.* Retrieved from http://www.projectsmart.co.uk/docs/chaos-report.pdf.

2

e-Leadership for Projects

INTRODUCTION

What happens to the leadership theories studied throughout the 20th century in the new virtual and global business environment? For example, how can the virtual project manager lead using management by walking around (MBWA) in a modern organization? Peters and Waterman [1] popularized MBWA back in 1982. This management approach encourages leaders to get out from behind their desks and go watch the employees work, to walk the halls and visit other offices, or stop to "catch up" at the water cooler. By doing this, the manager can observe who is working well and who is not and react to employees' positive or negative behaviors with actions, body language, and face-to-face conversation. MBWA managers are also able to show that this is their management style and expect others to model it.

It is no longer possible to physically watch employees work, walk the halls, shake hands, or visit at the water cooler in our modern work environment. Handy [2] asks: "Out of sight, foremost in mind. How do you manage people whom you don't regularly see?" MBWA now may need to be achieved by listening, reading, implementing ideas, distributing results [3], and instant messaging versus stopping by each employee's desk to visit. The virtual water cooler may become a wiki or website specifically designed to help create a shared identity for the team. Photos, ideas, links, and information beyond the team project can become important ways to bond the dispersed team members and help them feel less isolated.

How does a project manager shake hands virtually? During Roman times, the handshake assured that no knife was hidden in the sleeve of the other person. Modern handshaking has evolved as a way to show power or submission and nonverbal assurance. Is this lost in the virtual world? The objective of the physical handshake, to build trust, might be delivered by the e-leader through a video chat. By inviting several team members to the chat and starting with a welcoming message directed to each person, the e-leader begins to "shake hands." Inviting them to move their computer camera around to show their office and work area helps eliminate any "Is there a knife in your sleeve?" thinking. Encouraging comments and feedback can provide the small talk often associated with the traditional handshake.

And what about the Trait Theory model for leadership from the 1970s? The trait approach attempted to identify character traits of effective leaders. It was a popular theory validated by research that provided a yardstick approach to measuring leadership traits. Somewhat subjective in nature, the early model attempted to relate physical traits to effective leadership. But on a virtual team, physical traits are no longer important. Height, race, body size, hairstyle, gender, age, attractiveness—these physical traits do not transmit over the wires in the virtual world. The newer trait approach model suggests a different set of traits—such as drive, motivation, honesty and integrity, self-confidence, cognitive ability, knowledge of business, and charisma [4]. These traits are valuable for the virtual leader, changing this theory to better fit the 21st century.

"They say 'you either got it, or you don't,' but when it comes to charisma, you don't have to have it—you can learn it" [5]. *Charismatic leaders* influence by inspiring support and acceptance from others [6]—but can charisma be transmitted electronically? Charismatic leadership behaviors [7] could transfer to nontraditional project leadership. Table 2.1 portrays the three elements of charismatic leadership.

It appears that these behaviors would translate to our modern world of virtual and global organizations. The charismatic virtual leader needs to be able to share a clear vision, excite others to act, and empower the

TABLE 2.1

Three Elements of Charismatic Leadership

Envision the Future	Energize Others	Enable Others
Share a clear vision	Show enthusiasm	Be supportive
Set high expectations	Express confidence	Be empathetic
Model positive behaviors	Demonstrate success	Express confidence in others

members of the project team. Charismatic leadership behaviors may be valuable in a virtual environment. Maybe what is old can be new again?

Traditional leadership theories, studied by astute business and master of business administration (MBA) students, often do not compute in the virtual environment. Even Peter Drucker [8], considered a guru of leadership and management, suggests that the assumptions of management begun in the 1930s now need to be unlearned and might even be counterproductive. Today's dynamic organizations require e-leadership and the ability to adapt traditional management and leadership theories to the virtual work environment. This chapter attempts to meld traditional and outdated theories that often appear disconnected from the 21st century workplace with practical applications of those theories for today's virtual project managers.

DEFINING E-LEADERSHIP

Management throughout a project requires solving technical problems using knowledge, procedures, and skills. Management involves routine tasks using prescribed interventions, such as project planning, monitoring, and controlling. The field of organizational behavior defines *leadership* as "the ability to influence a group toward the achievement of goals" [9]. Leadership styles have been well studied and researched. Early leadership studies were developed using traditional, collocated work arrangements in mind.

e-Project management identifies the "extensive application of electronic technology to project management" [10] tools and techniques and is different from e-leadership because it does not include leadership in the definition. Management, as discussed above, involves routine tasks using prescribed interventions and does not include many of the competencies and abilities that leaders need to motivate and influence teams to higher levels of achievement. *e-Leadership* refers to true leadership of teams in today's nontraditional virtual business environment [11]. e-Leadership takes place in an environment where work is conducted electronically through information technology [12]. Narrowing the definition of the *e* in e-leadership by just electronic technology may itself be a dated concept. Instead, the *e* in e-leadership in the 21st century may stand for *evolving*—a

Then

"electronic" –
leading is
conducted
electronically
using technology

Now

"evolving" – leading in
the ever-changing global
business environment is
constantly evolving

FIGURE 2.1
Defining the "e" in "e-leadership."

reflection of our current, ever-changing global business environment and understanding of leadership (Figure 2.1).

Project leadership must be adaptive, find solutions, challenge the status quo, and often change procedure [13]. The type of leadership e-project managers must demonstrate for successful virtual team management is different from traditional project team management [14]. Understanding appropriate leadership styles for virtual project teams and the transition toward new leadership styles is an important part of managing human resources in organizations and successful virtual project management. Emerging e-leadership roles and management concepts for virtual teams include multiple leadership models, and their application is an important part of our evolving virtual organizational behavior.

Traditional project management requires both management and leadership skills, and virtual project management requires both e-project management and e-leadership skills. In the virtual project environment, the effective e-manager/leader needs to be able to apply as many different management, leadership, and communication styles as needed to bring the project to successful completion.

APPLICATION OF TRADITIONAL LEADERSHIP MODELS AND THEORIES TO VIRTUAL PROJECT MANAGEMENT

Control-Related Leadership

"The research is clear, and has been known in social science circles for decades: Carrot-and-stick thinking is, at its core, a control method—and people always resist being controlled. Even if they don't openly resist, people resent being coerced into certain behaviors" [15]. Control often has a negative connotation when linked to management behaviors, but leadership involves some degree of responsibility for influencing the behavior of workers [16]. Control-related leadership is defined as leading by tasks but also includes motivating, providing role clarity, setting clear goals and priorities, and giving good directions.

Control-related leadership has been linked to effective virtual team management. Konradt and Hoch [17] examined leadership roles and showed that the task leadership function was "rated as significantly more important to virtual team effectiveness than people leadership function" and "that managers in virtual teams viewed control-related roles as more appropriate for virtual team success and performance than non-control-related roles." Similar goal-related concepts can be found in management by objectives (MBO) studies. In the MBO model, management and employees agree to the goals of the organization and work in a participative culture to reach them. Previous studies found that control-related leadership strategies were positively related to virtual team success [18].

Research results show that control-related leadership roles correlate to virtual team success and performance [19]. A field study of two large companies in Germany showed that effective virtual team management practices included setting clear goals, tasks, and outcome interdependencies [20]. It found that the higher the quality of goal-setting processes and task interdependence, the more effective the virtual team. The implication is that e-leaders focus on high-quality goal setting and high task interdependence, and use team-based rewards to produce the best results from virtual teams. Hooijberg and Choi [21] found that the goal achievement role (attainment of goals, setting clear goals, and coordinating work) had a strong relationship with the perception of leadership effectiveness. Yet another study indicates that the task-motivated leadership style for shorter projects would appear to be effective [22]. The task-motivated leader focuses on planning, scheduling, roles, responsibilities and accountability, and task achievement. The task-motivated leader generally rewards task accomplishment and performance versus a more relationship-motivated leadership style that might use interpersonal relationships to measure performance and success. Organizations and executives using control-related leadership models need to know the tenure of projects and ensure that the project leaders' styles are appropriately matched to the term of the project.

In the 21st century, leadership is no longer perceived as power and control over people. Now optional, more popular, exciting, and challenging leadership models are in vogue. Several modern leadership theories posit that true leadership starts with giving away power and demonstrating vulnerability [23]. Control, as previously defined as leading by tasks and motivating work, can be shared within the virtual team. Although the project manager in the virtual environment is ultimately responsible for the project deliverable, the ability to share task control within the team to develop team members and increase engagement in the virtual work may be a viable alternative. Empowering virtual team members is an option to control-related leadership.

Leadership through Empowerment

Empowerment is leadership that encourages team members to work, make decisions, solve problems, and take appropriate actions autonomously through self-management. As one virtual project manager (anonymous) affirmed: "You can't micromanage a virtual team. For them to become fully engaged you must provide them with a sense of ownership." Empowerment is dependent upon a company cultural attitude that includes education about the organization and what is really happening in the organization, operational consistency, a proven process, loyalty, and trust [31]. It is often necessary for the virtual leader to provide motivational incentives, set objectives and vision, and develop an appropriate climate or tone for the virtual team [32]. Highlighting these organizational cultural behaviors may increase the availability of leadership through empowerment within the virtual team. The e-leader can do this by increasing the amount and detail of information shared with employees. Providing statistics, charts, graphs, and databases that give employees open access to company information, meeting regularly with employees regarding business issues and answering questions, and coaching employees to increase participation in organizational improvement can empower employees to self-manage. Team norms and organizational culture can be influencers on the success for teams that self-manage. These spoken or implied "rules" provide the basis for how the group will function and can be strong motivators for self-management and empowerment within the team.

Virtual team leaders need to be proactive in providing clear direction and specific goals to encourage each team member to monitor their own performance and self-regulate their work to be successful [33]. To do this, the leader develops rules, guidelines, and habitual routines for the team. Self-managing teams of 10–15 individuals usually report higher levels of job satisfaction [34].

The emergence of more than one leader may be the result of the virtual situation or environment of the empowered globally dispersed team, and virtual project managers must recognize that this might happen. A virtual project manager (anonymous) expressed these thoughts on how empowerment might lead to emergent leaders in a virtual project team: "Managing a team with more than two people is not an easy task because of the fact that sub-teams will emerge from the bigger team and this existence of smaller teams in a team have [sic] its challenges—and opportunities if well-managed. Nobody is an island on his or her own and projects are easier to execute where there is more than one collaborators [sic], especially with mutual understanding and team spirit." The results of a recent study [35] demonstrated that virtual teams may identify more than one leader. When identifying emergent leaders, regardless of whether a leader was assigned or not, the team members in the study considered perceived amounts of communication, intelligence, and encouraging behaviors as competencies that led them to identify emergent leaders within the team. Encouraging behaviors include showing others concern for them and their personal improvement—without question or criticism. Individuals who show encouraging behaviors often become emergent leaders by providing a supportive, positive climate that inspires others to self-improve and self-manage. The ability for team members to be recognized as leaders online can be seen as a direct result of empowerment of these individuals by the assigned virtual project manager.

Transformational and Transactional Leadership Styles

Transformational and transactional leadership characteristics are common management styles for virtual teams. *Transformational* leaders are defined as leaders who motivate and inspire followers to work. The transformational leader characteristics include the following:

1. Leading by example
2. Inspiring through articulating vision
3. Leading ethically, with integrity and optimism
4. Showing a willingness to take risks and responsibility to achieve the vision
5. Being proactive and confident

Transactional leaders are defined as leaders who encourage followers to complete goals by clearly identifying roles and setting vision [24], similar to control-related task leadership. In a study to determine virtual team leadership behaviors in projects, the results were divided into five major behaviors closely related to transactional leadership characteristics [25]:

1. Ability to provide role and expectation clarity and good communications
2. Willingness to work along with the team
3. Relationship-building skills
4. Ability to lead effective team meetings
5. Strong project management

Many e-leadership behaviors can be identified and linked to both transformational and transactional leadership styles. Leaders who inspire goals for virtual teams reflect the transformational-style motivational skills. Providing role and expectation clarity for virtual teams reflects the contingent reward factor of transactional-style leadership.

An interesting study by Kahai and Avolio [26] reviewed the effects of transactional versus transformational leadership styles on virtual groups challenged with the ethics of copying copyrighted software. Transformational leaders attempted to motivate the anonymous virtual team members to aspire to higher-order needs and values and fulfill their personal aspirations, stating that they would learn from their discussion about copying software by working together to arrive at a better conclusion. Transactional leaders attempted to motivate the anonymous virtual team members by highlighting the contractual exchanges involved and emphasizing what results would be derived from the information exchanges on the topic (such as a listing of ideas, completing the task, and getting credit for the discussion). The results showed that the teams working with transformational leaders were more likely to challenge the copying of copyrighted material. Those virtual team members working with the transactional leaders were more in favor of copying the copyrighted software. The transactional leadership led the group toward the contingent reward factor. A contingent reward system is based on meeting specific goals, using frequent reviews to motivate employees toward receiving rewards such as an extra vacation day, monetary bonuses, or other incentives. The transformational leadership led the group toward a higher level of analysis, with verbal accolades, praise, and compliments as effect motivators.

Motivation can be enhanced by providing challenges and recognition, and rewarding responsibility and creativity [27]. Communicating the vision can be achieved through a well-developed project charter, developing emotional buy-in and ownership of the vision within the team, and using the vision to guide and direct the work [28]. Inspiring followers to work and motivating followers to complete goals by clearly identifying roles and setting a vision are skills that can be learned. Training on transformational and transactional leadership skills and when each style is appropriate can provide an opportunity to apply these skills in real work situations. Developing training programs for virtual leaders and virtual project team members may increase team performance [29]. Leaders can be taught skills [30] and learn the leadership techniques that can be most effective in virtual team management.

Contingency School of Leadership

The *contingency school of leadership* emphasizes matching leadership style to the leadership situation. In Fiedler's [36] seminal book, he attempts to relate leadership style directly to situational variables. His significant contribution to leadership theory was his focus on situational variables as moderating influences. With this leadership style, the leader adopts the appropriate style for the circumstance to influence the performance of subordinates [37]. The leader uses a least-preferred co-worker (LPC) scale to determine which leadership style is most appropriate, but the model lacks the ability to holistically assess team members [38]. The LPC scale uses a bipolar set of 18 to 25 adjectives to rank the person the leader would most prefer to work with versus the person the leader would least prefer to work with. The resulting ranking would indicate whether the leader would respond with a human relations orientation (focusing on interpersonal relationships) or a task orientation (focusing on successful task performance). The virtual leader, depending upon a contingency style of leadership, is deficient in the ability to relate leadership style to the individual by focusing solely on relating leadership to the task, situation, or circumstance because in the virtual environment circumstances influencing performance are constantly fluctuating. For this reason, the contingency style in the virtual environment is less effective than the situational leadership style.

Situational Leadership Styles

The *situational leadership* style assumes that effective leaders can develop and adopt certain styles or behaviors depending upon the needs of the project and team. Situational leadership theory can provide the opportunity for the project manager to analyze the different patterns of leadership behavior and how this range of behaviors could determine the type of leadership needed to affect short- and long-range objectives [39]. Determining the degree of authority used by the project manager and the degree of freedom experienced by the virtual team members, the situational leadership-style continuum helps determine the behaviors needed. By adjusting the leadership style to fit the developmental needs of the employee, the leader can recognize more influence and effectiveness in changing the behavior(s) of the employee. The ability to adapt leadership style to the situation, team member, project, and ever-changing global environment of virtual project management can be essential to the success of the virtual project.

Hersey and Blanchard's [40] life-cycle theory of leadership can assist the project manager in adjusting to the maturity of the team member and becoming more flexible in what type of leadership behavior is needed, depending upon the needs of the individual. They used multiple dimensions—task/production oriented and people oriented—and the variable *maturity* scaled from most mature to most immature to develop a situational-style leadership model (telling, selling, participating, delegating) dependent upon workers' maturity. Using a telling or directing style would require the leader to make decisions and be very involved with managing the employee. Telling and directing would be used with the immature or new employee or employee who needs close supervision to guide them toward the best behaviors. This type of micromanagement may be necessary for the new virtual team member who is just learning how to manage time and work in the virtual environment. Selling or coaching the employee would be the style used for the employee who is more advanced, has some virtual work experience, and is able to provide input but still requires the leader to be involved and make final decisions. For a more mature employee, the leader may adopt a more participating and supporting role. This involves giving the employee more responsibility, including the ability to make decisions. The virtual employee with experience may be a good candidate for participative and supportive leadership. The most mature employee, who knows and understands the work and is very experienced in the virtual work environment, is managed at the delegating level. At this level, the situational leader is the least involved, giving the employee the responsibility to choose tasks and perform with little supervision. Adopting the life-cycle theory of leadership model, the e-leader may help control loss of mature, experienced virtual team members in the global environment and encourage development in newer, less experienced virtual team members.

Decision Tree Approach

The Vroom *Decision Tree Approach* [41] can help the project manager understand the team members' level of participation in decision making to determine the degree of autocratic, consultative, or group-oriented leadership necessary. This approach prescribes leadership styles appropriate for the situation. It uses the following five leadership styles that are dependent upon the subordinate participation to determine the degrees of being autocratic, consultative, or group oriented when making leadership decisions:

1. The manager makes the decision alone.
2. The manager allows the group to define the problem and develop a solution.
3. The manager obtains input from the group members individually and then makes the decision.
4. The manager obtains input from the group and then makes the decision.
5. The manager presents the problem, facilitates group discussion, and allows the group to make the decision.

Situations shape how leaders behave and influence the consequences of leader behavior. An overview of this theory is valuable to the project manager in understanding the relationship between the need for participation and the need for leadership with both the on-site and virtual team members and assists in balancing the team relationships and work.

Toward the end of the 20th century, Slevin and Pinto [42] challenged traditional research on leadership with a similar decision tree model. They attempted to describe a cognitive approach to leadership to help project managers consciously select the correct leadership style. Their two-dimensional leadership model (information input and decision authority) recognized three main leadership decision styles (participative, delegation, and pressured). By *participative* they referred to

- Consulting
- Empowering
- Encouraging sharing power and democracy

Their model defined delegation as sharing power when team members are given responsibility and authority to make decisions otherwise made by the leader, and approval of decisions may or may not be required by the leader before the decision can be implemented. A pressured decision requires the manager to move quickly and act alone due to time restrictions, assuming that the team will accept the decision.

This theory suggests that the leader should match leadership style to the situation to be successful, and included several conclusions concerning project management and leadership style drawn from the presentation and discussion of their leadership model with "thousands of practicing managers." Their work in plotting leadership style with the level of participation by project team members could be used as a day-to-day working framework for modern project managers.

Agile Project Management

Agile project management provides a fresh approach to leading projects. Agile project management is not a particular methodology but rather a general philosophy on how a project can be approached [43]. Agile project management is a process in which all individuals in the project have equal weight and the contributions of each member are equally important [44]. Agile project management can be used for any type of project, but it addresses a particular need for information technology (IT) products. Projects involving technology often change so fast that in a longer-term project methodology the software or IT solutions that are written into the requirements could potentially be outdated before the testing begins. Incremental iterations, specific processes, self-management, and a focus on eliminating waste define some of the major elements of the agile model. The mature agile team member is skilled and willing, responsible and focused. Many agile projects involve virtual team members, but the majority of agile projects are with traditional teams.

Agile process development does not rely as heavily on documentation as traditional waterfall project management. A simple document stating the client's requirements for functionality can replace pages of waterfall model documentation and details. Documentation is not a requirement during the agile process. Programmers can move on to the next task or step prior to documentation being completed. Interaction with the clients allows programmers to receive feedback during the entire development process. During the agile process, meetings (called *stand-ups*) are held to discuss issues. The challenge of stand-ups for nontraditional teams is often addressed by using technology to virtually meet regularly, such as online meetings or videoconferencing. The nature and urgency of these meetings require clear, quick communication—often making electronic face-to-face communication necessary. The period of development in agile project management is called a *sprint*. After a sprint, the client determines whether the software has the functionality that is required. Then the software is tested and integrated, and it is determined whether another sprint is required. At that time, the team gets back together, examines the new functionality requirements, and starts the process all over again. The repeating of sprints continues until the software contains all of the functionality that the client requires [45].

The agile team generally shares leadership throughout this process. The cross-functional team, not a project leader, determines the tasks or functionality that each member is going to complete. The team also determines the way in which the software is going to be written to achieve the functionality that the client requires [46].

The five phases of agile project management [47], all of which can be shared and led by various team members, are as follows:

- Envision—Formulate a vision of the product to be delivered and convey that to all involved, including stakeholders, customers, product managers, and team members
- Speculate—Create a backlog and feature-based release plan
- Explore—Deliver product stories, including risk mitigation and managing customer and stakeholder interactions
- Adapt—Review and modify deliverables based on feedback from the customers and technical teams
- Close—Close the iteration and pass the lessons learned forward to the next iteration or development team

Benefits of agile methodology might include getting the product to the market faster, increased operational efficiencies, reduced financial expenditures, and a final product with minimal revisions required [48]. Leaders can claim several business objectives that substantiate the use of the agile process in IT projects, such as continuous innovation; product, process, and human resource adaptability; and reliable results [49]. The major challenge with virtual agile project management is in the need for immediate interaction and communication between project team members and the client. Because stand-ups are frequent and often impromptu, and sprints are completed quickly, virtual agile projects require advanced technology to be successful. Of the five phases of agile project management, Envision, Speculate, and Close are most adaptable to the virtual environment and can be completed using asynchronous technology, such as shared databases and e-mail. The Explore and Adapt phases require creative options and often synchronous virtual communication, such as e-meetings, texting, and instant messaging (Figure 2.2).

Servant Leadership and Grateful Leadership

The servant-leader shares power by delegating and engaging in participative decision making, puts the needs of others first, and attempts to encourage employees to perform to their maximum potential. *Servant leadership* was seen as a long-term application and often not applied to virtual project management because projects traditionally are defined as temporary, with a definite beginning and end. Recently, a study found that the statistical differences between the perception of servant leadership in virtual and face-to-face teams was minimal [50]. Despite the lack

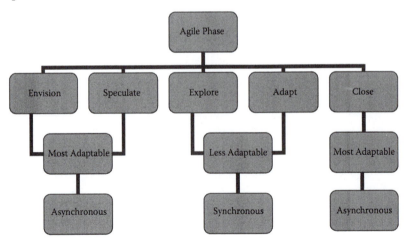

FIGURE 2.2
Adapting agile project management in the virtual environment.

of face-to-face interaction, servant leadership is seen as increasingly viable and has become a critical part of online project management because of the high amount of trust that is built between the project leader and team members in the virtual project environment [51]. A servant-leader's success in the virtual organization depends upon trust, personal connections, and collaboration. Developing a sense of belonging to the organization by the employee and a perception of value to the project and the project team will help the servant-leader build this type of relationship. In turn, job satisfaction and performance are improved and projects can achieve higher success. Virtual servant-leaders can use multiple virtual communication avenues to interact with their team members, such as social media involving video, pictures, and audio [52]. Virtual technologies that encourage one-on-one interaction, direct face-to-face virtual meetings, and personalized messages can be successful in establishing the interpersonal connections necessary for servant leadership to be successful on the virtual level.

A newer model, called *grateful leadership* [53], echoes the original servant-leader theory. This model stresses the importance of the leader expressing appreciation; acknowledging, supporting, and engaging employees; and having personal relationships with employees. The benefits of grateful leadership are similar and show that it may create improved relationships, a positive work environment, and improved productivity. It may also help engage and retain top talent and provide increased commitment to the organization. Grateful leadership can be used to make immediate changes to the team culture that can enhance productivity and satisfaction. It is a method by which simple gestures of timely appreciation can replace expensive employee bonuses and reward systems without adding expense to the organization or to the project budget. In the virtual environment, these gestures of appreciation can be delivered using the same technologies and techniques as with servant leadership.

Models of Team Development

Memorized by most business and MBA students, the Tuckman [54] stages of team development (forming, storming, norming, performing, and adjourning) adapt easily to traditional teams but do not adapt well to the virtual environment. Lacking collocation and predefined work arrangements, the virtual team does not have the luxury of working through the traditional sequential five stages to achieve good communication,

TABLE 2.2

Virtual Team Development

Stage	Activities
Inception	Generating goals, ideas, procedures
Problem solving	Addressing technical issues and problems and determining solutions
Conflict resolution	Collaborating on different approaches
Execution	Performing work

performance, and production and determine effective interactive work roles. Some norms and rules in small groups are stated verbally in the traditional environment, while other norms and rules are implied or are learned through observation of the behavior of other group members. The virtual team needs a new model to define how it interacts, resolves conflict, makes decisions, communicates, and builds trust and relationships.

The new model for the dynamics of virtual team development [55] involves four stages, as illustrated in Table 2.2, Virtual Team Development. One of the powerful differences in the virtual model is that the stages are not sequential, nor is every stage required. A mature team may move quickly from one stage to another, eliminate stages, or return to a stage whenever necessary. For example, a team that is repeating work may have fewer issues and be able to move directly from stage one to stage four. This enables the flexibility and adaptability necessary when working in a global, nontraditional team environment. Should a new member join the virtual team, it is possible for one or more of the seasoned team members to return to the earlier stage of *inception* or *problem solving* to bring the new member up to speed. Project management best practices encourage the use of a team charter that clearly defines how the team will resolve conflict, so *conflict resolution* in the virtual team environment can be accomplished quickly and efficiently whenever necessary in the team's development. *Execution* does not mean completion of the project but refers to the actual performing of work by the team toward the deliverable(s) of the project. Should the team need to move into the *problem-solving* stage during *execution*, this more flexible model encourages that move because it is a nonlinear model of team development.

The ARCS Model

The *ARCS model* [56] of motivation is applicable to the leadership of e-projects and provides a fresh alternative to traditional models of leadership.

Using a problem-solving approach, it is designed to motivate, stimulate, and sustain motivation. The acronym stands for—

- Attention
- Relevance
- Confidence
- Satisfaction

The premise for the e-leader is to use ARCS to motivate team members to perform better and more consistently on their own. It is especially useful when the leader needs to encourage the project team to learn and explore solutions to succeed. Table 2.3 details how this model could be applied to virtual project management.

TABLE 2.3

ARCS Model

ARCS	Description	Application for Virtual Leaders
Attention	• Gain interest • Stimulate information-seeking behavior • Maintain interest	• Use novel, surprising, and interesting communications to get the team involved; help the team members get to know each other personally; share stories about virtual project work • Pose questions and generate problem solving; nurture thinking; encourage conversation • Vary the types of communications to the team (e-mail, virtual meetings, documents, teleconferences, personal phone calls, etc.); encourage relationships within the team
Relevance	• Familiarity • Goal orientation • Motive matching	• Use templates and standardized forms; provide e-databases and knowledge-sharing technology; use a common methodology; acknowledge team members' experience and expertise • Communicate clear goals and objectives; determine accountability for tasks; visualize success for the project • Adapt a leadership style that matches the situations that arise and individuals on the team; provide cooperative activities; lead as a positive role model

(continued)

TABLE 2.3

ARCS Model (continued)

ARCS	Description	Application for Virtual Leaders
Confidence	• Success expectations • Opportunities • Feedback	• Provide clear requirements for accountability and responsibility for each team member • Provide training and challenges for team members; set standards for success; encourage skill and competency building • Include frequent feedback and support to motivate the virtual team
Satisfaction	• Intrinsic reinforcement • Extrinsic rewards • Equity	• Place value on team relationships and provide opportunities to build virtual relationships; encourage personal development and growth • Provide incentives, rewards, and kudos; provide opportunities for the project work to be presented to appropriate audiences • Maintain consistent standards and consequences for task accomplishment; complete a Lessons Learned session for the project

Entrepreneurial Leadership

"Some people suggest that today's project leaders should think of the project as a business enterprise and manage the project as a business," says Mayer [57]. *Entrepreneurial leadership* combines the characteristics of successful leaders and entrepreneurs. The primary characteristics of entrepreneurial leadership involve vision, problem solving, decision making, risk taking, and strategic initiatives [58]. As global competition increases, the need for entrepreneurial leadership may parallel the need for organizations to think more strategically and take more risks to stay competitive. This theory has increased in popularity, spawning the term *intrapreneurship* [59] for those leaders in large corporations who exhibit the characteristics of entrepreneurial leadership. Research shows that the successful entrepreneurial leader is able to motivate and is achievement oriented. The entrepreneurial leader is also creative, flexible, patient, persistent, a risk-taker, and a visionary [60].

The traditional entrepreneur tends to manage tasks alone, but the virtual entrepreneur is characterized as a leader who is able to organize others to get things done by jobbing the work out or hiring virtual employees. The entrepreneurial leader possesses many of the characteristics of other leadership styles, yet has the distinguishing characteristic of being successful with start-up projects [61]. For new projects or information technology (IT) projects, these characteristics can be powerful in a leader.

Managing a virtual project team may indeed be managing a team of virtual entrepreneurs. Many virtual workers are themselves entrepreneurial by nature. New research indicates that statistics on job deficits do not accurately reflect today's business environment, which are due to a number of factors, including technology and globalization [62]. Progressive companies have created the platforms and infrastructures that support freelance entrepreneurs, including project managers and team members. Teams blended with full-time traditional employees and contingent, freelance entrepreneurs may predict the project environment of the future.

Extreme Agility

Adaptive environments do not follow rational, structured rules and often require different leadership strategies. Many virtual teams work in adaptive environments or face adaptive situations. Adaptability is no longer considered a competency that is "nice to have," but it is necessary as a competitive advantage for any leader and organization. The *extreme agility* model, which is not the same as the agile project management philosophy, focuses on several skills that are crucial for the success of the 21st century virtual leader. Extreme agility posits that highly agile leaders are able to manage change effectively and use change as an opportunity to increase competitive advantage [63]. The agility factor refers to "the characteristics and behaviors that enable individuals and organizations to interact successfully with extreme change, to survive in a world in which the rate of change is increasing and unexpected events are becoming more radical in nature" [64]. The term *agility* is broken down by letter as an acronym suggesting that agility is always—

- A—apparent (clarity of project)
- G—grounded (data to support the objective)
- I—invested (resources and value added support)
- L—linked in (stakeholder buy-in, allies, coalition)
- I—informed (strategic management of obstacles)
- T—tactical (implementation plan)
- Y—yielding (contingency plan)

FIGURE 2.3
Agile leader characteristics.

The theory suggests seven characteristics of agile leaders, which can be modified to suggest seven key agility factors for virtual project managers. Figure 2.3, agile leader characteristics [65], shows the key characteristics identified by this theory.

Modifying these characteristics to the virtual project manager, the application could be as follows:

- Clarifying Goals: The e-leader must have the ability to clearly communicate the project mission and objectives.
- Analyzing: The virtual leader must be able to manage the team's expertise. The leader also needs to encourage a broad sphere of analysis for the project, including benchmarking; reviewing company data, lessons learned, and knowledge bases; utilizing subject matter experts; and involving key stakeholders.
- Collaborating: Mindfully communicating with a broad network within and outside the organization, the leader needs to ensure the approval and support of allies for the project by building relationships. The leader also needs to connect the vision of the project to the team members and the work.
- Optimizing: To optimize leadership, leaders should continue to expand their own knowledge, expertise, and contacts; provide training for

team members; solicit buy-in for the project; and optimize technology to the advantage of the project.

- Strategizing: Similar to the traditional project manager, the virtual project manager should be able to identify and remove obstacles for the team, negotiate strategies to solve problems, and champion the project.
- Contingency Planning: Leaders should incorporate risk management plans, be knowledgeable on change management, and be prepared to launch contingency and mitigation plans to minimize negative impacts.
- Executing: Using project management skills and techniques, the virtual project manager needs to manage the daily progress and work of the project, adjust the work breakdown structure, and monitor and control the work.

NEGATIVE E-LEADERSHIP APPROACHES

Authoritarian Leadership Style

Authoritarian managers lead by force, resource control, or power [66]. The authoritarian manager will dictate policies and procedures, determine team goals, and attempt to direct and control activities. The dictatorship-like power the authoritarian manager uses is a negative influence to the project team. "In the virtual environment, there is no such thing as a de facto leader. The manager has to become the leader through influence, not through authority or implied right" [67].

However, power used constructively can be a significant factor in contributing to a win-win environment for project teams. French and Raven [68] suggest five bases of power: expert, referent, reward, legitimate, and coercive/punishment. Expert power can be used to create a win-win environment and centers around mutual respect. This includes respect for the individual and for the individual's knowledge, expertise, and experience. Referent power, similar to expert, involves the personal feelings that the project manager and project team member have for each other—the desire for association, personal relationship, admiration, and closeness/attraction. Expert and referent power are related to positive subordinate behaviors. Win-win environments increase value and influence professionals to cooperate for the greater good and mutual benefit [69]. The project manager, traditional or virtual, should describe a win-win vision that the entire team feels comfortable with and that reflects and serves individual interests as much as possible [70]. Obviously, the project manager should lead by motivating, communicating effectively, encouraging participation in decision making, and creating a clear and compelling vision for the project team regardless of the type of project team [71]. Project leaders should be chosen for leadership ability in addition to technical expertise—a combination leading to expert power [72]. The project manager should respect the talents of the team and consider them as allies, creating a bond between the project manager and team member [73], reflecting referent power. Creating operating agreements (team guidelines) that encourage creative, team-based interaction reflect a win-win environment [74]. Interpersonal skills and building relationships with team members are critical to expert and referent power.

Reward, coercive/punishment, and legitimate power are generally negatively related to leadership [75]. Reward power could be used to create a win-win environment by providing kudos, benefits, special help, or positive performance ratings to those project team members who contribute to project success (completion of deliverables on time, in scope, in budget, and with quality). But, rewards are usually one-time and not necessarily sustainable, especially in the virtual environment. Legitimate power refers to the influence that the project manager might have over the project team member and involves the values, norms, influence, and standards within the organization and the project manager/team member relationship. These influencers are difficult to enforce in the virtual environment. Coercive/punishment power is not a win-win option in any work environment.

When evaluating the bases of power for virtual project application, reward and coercive/punishment power should not be considered. Legitimate power involves the status of the leader in the organizational hierarchy and how that power is carried out according to the culture of the organization. Evaluating the traditional hierarchical organizational chart, the leader would be above the subordinates. In the virtual environment, opportunities for empowerment, expertise, and relationships often replace the traditional hierarchy of the nonvirtual business setting. Members of the virtual team cannot see the large, window office with its expensive leather chair and polished walnut desk. The virtual team cannot see the anecdotal evidence of leadership by legitimate power. Instead, the horizontal, nonhierarchical setting of the virtual environment provides a more global and shared view of the project and work. The structure of the virtual team involves a vertical structure where communication and shared knowledge take precedence over the status of the individual.

The more positive bases of power—expert and referent—are more applicable to virtual work. Expert power, focused on mutual respect and appreciation for the expertise and knowledge of the individual, and referent power, focused on the team relationships and the interpersonal relationships within the team, are the bases for several leadership styles that work well in the global and virtual business environment. Figure 2.4 reviews the bases of

| Base of Power | Characteristics | Application to Virtual Environment | | Applicable Leadership Models |
		Adaptable	Not Adaptable	
Most Effective				
Expert	Mutual respect, empowerment	X		• Leadership through empowerment • Transactional leadership • Situational leadership • Decision Tree Approach
Referent	Team cohesiveness, strong interpersonal relationships	X		• Situational leadership • Servant leadership • Grateful leadership • ARCS model • Extreme agility
Least Effective				
Reward	Short term		X	
Legitimate	Organizational status replaces leadership		X	
Coercive/ punishment	Negative reinforcement, reprimands, penalties		X	

FIGURE 2.4

Application of the five bases of power to virtual leadership. (From Podsakoff, P. M., & Scheiesheim, C. (1985). *Psychological Bulletin.* 97(3). 387–411.)

power, their characteristics, the applicability of each to the virtual environment, and the type of leadership model or style that may be suited to each.

Laissez-Faire Leadership

The *laissez-faire leadership* style is characterized by the general failure of the leader to take responsibility for managing. The meaning of the term itself appears to be an oxymoron—*noninterference* (laissez-faire) and *providing direction* (leadership) are almost polar opposites. In a virtual environment, the lack of leadership creates chaos, isolation, and inefficiency. In project management, the laissez-faire leadership style is ineffective in motivating virtual employees and providing job satisfaction or enrichment. Although this leadership style is considered hands-off and is designed to allow team members to make decisions and self-manage, it lacks the leadership needed for project teams to be productive, particularly virtual project teams. Unlike other theories that involve empowering the team, this model provides very little guidance, complete freedom for the team to make whatever decisions they would like, no help in removing obstacles for the team, and no input from management on solving problems. Projects under this type of leadership often move out of scope or lose the vision for the project, and deadlines can be missed. In project management, the project manager is responsible for the project being in scope, on time, in budget, and delivered as a quality product. The laissez-faire leadership model does not allow for enough participation by the project manager to effectively achieve these goals, especially in the virtual project environment. Laissez-faire leadership has been shown to increase role conflict, role ambiguity, team conflict, and the chances for bullying and workplace stress among project team members [76].

Leader–Member Exchange Theory

The *Leader–Member Exchange Theory* of leadership identifies in- and out-groups that are treated positively and negatively, respectively. This theory, also known as the Vertical Dyad Linkage Model, explores how leaders and managers develop relationships with team members that can either contribute to growth or hold people back. In this model, the leader attempts to develop and reinforce certain team members (the in-group), giving them the more interesting opportunities than the less-talented team members (the out-group) [77]. The intended result is that the in-group will achieve better results and higher job satisfaction [78]. However, the reality of this model is that it often results in tension and conflict within the team and a negative and unproductive work environment. It is not recommended for effective project management. As Whipple suggests, "Playing favorites is one of the most damaging problems in any group of people" [79]. True leadership takes into consideration each individual's needs, which often means not treating everyone the same. However, leaders who practice favoritism in the workplace have no chance to build a culture of trust—which is crucial to the success of a virtual project.

MOVING TOWARD MULTIPLE E-LEADERSHIP STYLES

Wiener wisely stated: "We have modified our environment so radically that we must modify ourselves in order to exist in this new environment" [80]. Virtual project management has become increasingly important and a necessity as the trend in virtual work teams continues. Leadership styles for managing virtual project teams are different from leadership roles for managing traditional, collocated teams. Recognizing the concepts of emerging e-leadership styles (such as agile project leadership, the new model for the dynamics of virtual team development, empowerment, agile leaders, and entrepreneurial leadership) for virtual project teams and their application is an important part of our evolving virtual organizational behavior. Quality leaders must be able to accept responsibility, lead, build teamwork, motivate, use technology, negotiate, facilitate, think critically, and communicate effectively [81] as well as to deliver the project on time, in scope, in budget, and with quality—quite a list for today's virtual project manager to accomplish.

Benefits of Multiple Leadership Styles in Virtual Projects

Management and leadership in the virtual environment differ in many ways but are not different in that team members need support, guidance, and encouragement. Regardless of traditional or virtual, most employees need to feel productive and valuable and want a positive relationship with management. The project manager's leadership style and competencies contribute to predict success, and organizations make decisions for appointment and deployment of project managers based upon these skill sets [82]. Understanding control-related leadership roles, using transformational and transactional leadership styles, empowering virtual project teams to self-manage, and incorporating situational and contingency leadership styles are some examples of leadership concepts for virtual teams that may be able to offer benefits to the organization by providing positive, successful leadership, resulting in better project deliverables. (See Figure 2.5, Applications of six leadership concepts for virtual teams.)

As one virtual project manager (anonymous) stated: "I believe the virtual project manager can be most effective by using the appropriate leadership style based on the competency of your team members, and not a one-size-fits-all approach. I believe all communications and leadership moments are unique and require adaptation. It is impossible to apply one of a fixed number of styles or approaches." The general conclusion is that multiple leadership styles can be appropriately applied to project management leadership [83]. As Baldoni [84] suggests, "One week things might be topsy-turvy; the next week things appear calm. The savvy leader is nimble enough to know when to wield a stick as well as when to wear the velvet glove." Applying multiple theories and research to virtual project management provides an improved approach for managing human resources. The application to human resource management is that this flexibility in leadership style can provide the key to profitable project work, satisfied team members, and continued organizational growth through successful virtual project deliverables. Leadership becomes a combination of the degree of virtualness (hybrid or truly virtual) and the leadership

Leadership Concept	Description	Application
Control related	Leads by tasks	Use a high-quality goal setting process
	Motivates	Encourage task interdependence
	Provides role clarity	Lead by task for shorter projects
	Sets clear goals and priorities	
	Gives good directions	

FIGURE 2.5
Applications of six leadership concepts for virtual teams.

(continued)

Leadership Concept	Description	Application
Transformational	Inspires followers to work	Clearly identify roles
		Set the project vision
Transactional	Motivates followers to complete goals	Use a well-developed project charter
	Clearly identifies roles	Develop emotional buy-in and ownership of the vision
	Reinforces the vision	Use the vision to guide and direct the work
Empowerment	Leads self-managed work teams	Develop rules, guidelines, and habitual routines
	Distributes leadership functions	Provide motivational incentives
		Set strong objectives and mission
		Develop an appropriate climate or tone
Situational	Adopts certain styles or behaviors	Be skilled in multiple leadership styles
	Adjusts to the maturity of the subordinate	Adopt the appropriate style dependent upon the experience and needs of the team member
Contingency	Matches leadership style to the activity/work	Be trained on multiple leadership styles
	Assigns workers to task-oriented or participative leaders	Remain flexible
	Adapts to environmental factors	Adapt and apply the appropriate leadership style as necessary
	Leads dependent upon the needs of the team	

FIGURE 2.5 (CONTINUED)

Applications of six leadership concepts for virtual teams.

role behaviors that influence the outcome of the group [85]. Leadership itself need not be limited to just one person or an official leader. We need to look at leadership in the virtual context as how the leadership role(s) work within the team to produce the most desired effect. Although virtual work may increase the need for procedure and advanced technology, leadership remains a primary need for moving the team forward with the work. The amount and type of that leadership remains dependent upon the team. In researching the role that leadership played in the success of a virtual investment group, Pauleen [86] found that leadership activities that were intended to motivate contribution and cooperation within the group did not contribute to the group's effectiveness. However, procedural leadership behaviors, such as task, technology, and information management, did benefit the group with the outcome of more successful portfolio values. Therefore, the amount and regulation of leadership input, combined with the type of input, can reflect upon the success of the virtual team. Research on effects of leadership and electronic communication, the effects of leadership and virtualness, and the effects of leadership and virtual team member relationships continues to evolve as we move further into the 21st century and an increasingly global project environment.

LOOKING AHEAD: CURRENT APPROACHES TO VIRTUAL COMMUNICATIONS

Flexibility in leadership style is a key to successful virtual projects. The successful e-leader is comfortable and knowledgeable with all effective and successful leadership models. The project manager needs to recognize that different people relate to different forms of e-leadership and, as a result, different forms of communication are necessary for different individuals. Chapter 3 of this book discusses one of the most important competencies of any successful virtual project management leadership style: communication. What are the current communication approaches and tools used by successful project managers in virtual projects? One virtual project manager (anonymous) interviewed suggests that communication for a virtual project manager is "... very similar to a nonvirtual PM—it's just that the mediums of communication are more limited." Are they? Are there advantages and disadvantages to communications for those leading and managing projects virtually? Application of the best practice communication techniques for virtual projects is covered in Chapter 3.

Case Study 2.1: Social Media Site Project

OVERVIEW

The key characteristics of the Social Media Site Project provide an example of a hybrid (virtual and collocated) project in need of effective leadership. The deliverable of the project is to produce an Internet website that can be used by all members of the division. A project manager at the main office of the organization currently manages this project. The project manager's leadership style is mixed, fluctuating between authoritarian and laissez-faire. The project manager has no experience or training in virtual project team management.

Because the project manager's leadership style fluctuates between authoritarian and laissez-faire, the entire project team pivots from "taking orders" to putting the project "on the back burner." With no experience or training in virtual project team management, the manager tends to forget the virtual team members and focuses entirely on the on-site project team located at the main office. The result is virtual team members who are out of the loop and on-site project team members who are overworked. Often when leading the on-site team and in interactions with the virtual members of the team (when they are not entirely ignored), the project manager is controlling and demanding. The result is tension and resentment by the team members. The project manager assumes that the virtual members have the same language, culture, time zones, and company culture as the collocated team, which surprises and insults the virtual team members.

The impact of the unsuccessful leadership of the project manager has resulted in poor virtual attendance at meetings, incomplete work, and missed deadlines. Confusion between virtual and collocated team members stems from the poor or absent communications by the project manager. Virtual team members are dissatisfied with the project, and many mature members have left the original team and been replaced by virtual members with less expertise and experience, weakening the project. The manager's inexperience in virtual project team management and focus on the on-site project team has resulted in virtual team members who feel lost and ignored and on-site team members who receive most of the workload, creating tension between the team members. This imbalance has affected the productivity and effectiveness of the team, and the project is behind schedule.

HUMAN RESOURCE MANAGEMENT

The Social Media Site Project provides challenges for human resource management in the areas of

- Productivity improvement
- Attracting and maintaining skilled team members
- Organizational project management capability

An understanding of each of these areas is necessary to develop solutions for an improved approach to leading and managing the human resources of the project.

PRODUCTIVITY IMPROVEMENT

Scholars continue to research whether job satisfaction (lacking in the Social Media Site Project team members), a primary dependent variable in organizational behavior, impacts employee productivity, absenteeism, and turnover. It is difficult to find research that supports a direct relationship between satisfaction and performance [1]. High levels of productivity do not necessarily mean high levels of job satisfaction [2], and little evidence exists that links productivity and satisfaction [3]. Factors such as reward systems for performance, salary levels, promotions, and incentives blur the issue.

ATTRACTING AND MAINTAINING A SKILLED WORKFORCE

Better research results are found in correlating job satisfaction and employee retention [4]. Several Social Media Site Project members have left the original team and been replaced by virtual members with less expertise and experience, causing delays to the project. Under an authoritarian leader, creativity is suppressed, which is one possible reason for the loss of experienced team members. One recent study provides data that show a significant path coefficient between a creative environment and turnover [5]. However, the study was challenged by incomplete definitive attributes of the job descriptions for employees and of *creative environment* because it was done in a university student setting. Other research addressed one result of the effects of the laissez-faire management on the Training Site team members, employee engagement [6]. This qualitative study found that high engagement levels were related to retention.

ORGANIZATIONAL PROJECT MANAGEMENT CAPABILITY

The *project success model* posits that to improve organizations' project performance, it is necessary to develop a culture in the organization that supports project management [7]. Support of project management in organizations tends to lead to successful projects. Select and measurable criteria can then be used to compare how projects support the organization [8]. This establishes a win-win situation between the project management and the organization. Aligning project management with business strategy can significantly enhance the achievement of organizational goals and strategies [9]. At the organization for the Social Media Site Project, the capability of project management is respected and well instituted, so changes within the virtual Social Media Site Project would be supported by the organization.

CHALLENGES FOR THE CURRENT LEADERSHIP STYLES USED FOR THE SOCIAL MEDIA SITE PROJECT

The authoritarian leader does not have an accurate self-image and is often insensitive to others' feelings and needs [10]. Moderate situational control is better suited to leaders who are relationship motivated than directive, controlling, and insensitive leaders (such as the Social Media Site Project manager) [11]. Virtual team leadership skills should include motivation; role, directional, and priority clarification; and behaviors to ensure telecommuter job satisfaction and virtual team success [12]. These behaviors are missing in the authoritarian and laissez-faire styles exhibited by the Social Media Site Project manager. The emergence of more than one leader may be the result of the situation or environment of this virtual team [13], and the Social Media Site Project manager must recognize this fact. Situations shape how leaders behave and influence the consequences of leader behavior [14].

The project manager's behavior of focusing on the in-house team and ignoring the virtual project team is somewhat similar to the Leader–Member Exchange Theory of leadership. Also known as the Vertical Dyad Linkage Model, this leadership style identifies in- and out-groups and they are treated positively and negatively, respectively. The intended result is that the in-group will achieve better results and higher job satisfaction [15]. The difficulty with this model is that it often results in tension and conflict between the groups, developing a negative and unproductive work environment, something that is evident in the Social Media Site Project and exacerbated by the fact that the team is a hybrid of virtual and collocated individuals.

RECOMMENDATIONS

By adopting a situational leadership style, this project manager could provide positive, successful leadership to the Social Media Site Project, resulting in better project deliverables and products. Situational leadership for the Social Media Site Project must reflect the understanding that virtual project management is different from traditional project management. Successful leadership of virtual project teams will encourage better virtual project deliverables, e-team members with high job satisfaction, and sustainable organizational growth through virtual work. By demonstrating situational leadership, the Social Media Site Project manager will be able to offer benefits to the organization by providing positive, successful leadership to the virtual project team. The result will be a project that is on time, in budget, and in scope, with quality project deliverables [16].

Changes need to be made to implement the new leadership style to more effectively manage the human resources for the project. Individuals look at change in terms of the effect upon themselves [17] and the value of the change from their perspective, often exhibiting resistance to change. Christensen, Marx, and Stevenson [18] suggest several strategies that can improve the management of human resources for the Social Media Site Project manager to effect successful and positive leadership change. Strategies to overcome resistance to change include providing management tools (training, operating procedures, and metrics), leadership tools (improved communication and a clearly communicated vision), and cultural tools (organizational patterns, norms, beliefs, rituals). These tools will enhance the trust needed to make and sustain change. Training and enhanced communication will help the project team adapt and understand. The changes to the leadership style for the Social Media Site Project will improve the efficiency of the project tasks and ultimately the deliverable of the virtual web project, moving the organization to a more competitive position in the market by providing the division with a website. But change is never easy, for management or the team.

CHANGE READINESS OF THE PROJECT MANAGER

A shift in paradigms is needed to move away from authoritarian and laissez-faire leadership into virtual project team leadership and the situational leadership style. Individuals are resistant to change because it often involves discomfort, stress, and conflict [19], and the project manager may be resistant to change. Because there may be resistance to changing leadership styles, the most appropriate change model for the project manager's supervisor at this organization to help the project manager change leadership styles would be Christensen, Marx, and Stevenson's [20] model. This project manager needs training in management (project management procedures and processes), leadership (communication), and cultural understanding (on-site versus virtual team norms and expectations).

CHANGE READINESS OF THE PROJECT TEAM

Positioning the project team to adapt to the project manager's new virtual project management situational leadership style will require the project manager's initiation. The project manager can play the role of a change agent [21]. The project manager's positive attitude and willingness to try new things in the new structure to create opportunities, flexibility, and patient, compassionate understanding with those who are having difficulty with the change(s) are valuable assets to the organization. The project manager can also involve stakeholders both professionally and emotionally to gain commitment to change [22]. Creating buy-in for the new environment should be an initial focus for the project manager. Part of change management is helping the team to define how the new ways are different and to identify the benefits and the obstacles. It may be helpful to have someone from upper management come talk with the project team about the benefits for the company. Open discussion regarding the differences between the old and new ways and involving the team in decisions will help move those who are negative about the change toward a more positive attitude by allowing them ownership and control of changes whenever possible.

CHANGE READINESS OF THE ORGANIZATION

Understanding resistance and managing change are important to the success of change management [23]. Effective change initiatives must include the human factor to be successful. The failure to deal with employee resistance, the organization's culture, management skills, communication, and top-level management visibility throughout the change are the main reasons why change efforts fail [24]. Creating buy-in should be an initial focus for the project manager and the project manager's supervisor, with support from upper management to relate the benefits for the company. Open discussion regarding leadership style differences will help move those who are negative toward a more positive attitude.

IMPLEMENTATION STRATEGIES FOR THE RECOMMENDATIONS

Implementation strategies for the recommendation include training and development in leadership skills and in virtual project team management for the project manager.

TRAINING AND DEVELOPMENT IN LEADERSHIP SKILLS

Although authoritarian leaders can acquire new skills and knowledge, they are often unable to apply them because self-insight is necessary for personal growth and development [25]. Educating the project manager on situational leadership will require providing the manager the time and resources to learn about situational leadership theory, do self-assessment, and begin to develop a strategy for adapting the approach to the virtual project. Because authoritarians have lower self-awareness and are not open to learning new things about themselves, the project manager may resist change [26]. Reassurance and encouragement will be necessary to transition the project manager to a different leadership style.

Situational leadership theory would provide the opportunity for the project manager to analyze the different patterns of leadership behavior and how this range of behaviors could determine the type of leadership needed to affect short- and long-range objectives [27]. By determining the degree of authority used by the project manager and the degree of freedom experienced by the virtual team members, the continuum could help determine the behaviors needed. The project manager would improve virtual team relationships and communication by becoming aware of the environment, virtual culture, subordinates, and self-awareness, and behaving appropriately with insight and flexibility according to these perceptions. The life-cycle theory of leadership [28] would assist the project manager in adjusting to the maturity of the team members and in becoming more flexible in what type of leadership behavior is needed, depending upon the needs of each individual. This model could help control the exodus of mature, experienced virtual team members from the team. The Vroom Decision Tree Approach [29] could help the project manager understand the team members' level of participation to determine the degree of autocratic, consultative, or group-oriented leadership necessary. An overview of this theory would be valuable to the project manager in understanding the relationship between the need for participation and the need for leadership with both the on-site and virtual team members and assisting in balancing the team relationships and work.

TRAINING AND DEVELOPMENT FOR VIRTUAL PROJECT MANAGEMENT

Managing project teams in a virtual environment poses challenges to those accustomed to traditional work groups in functional organizations. In an organization experiencing resource restrictions and growth that involves an evolution to cross-functional virtual project teams, interpersonal skills and the ability to be an agent of change are important skills for the project manager. The project manager's inability to lead the project team through the challenges of working on a virtual team presents an ongoing untold risk to this project. To be successful in obtaining the goal of a fully functioning virtual team, the project manager needs to have additional training in communication skills. Virtual and hybrid teams are harder to manage than collocated teams, and communication is the primary challenge [30]. The virtual team members rely upon technology to communicate—e-mail, voice mail, teleconferences, and videoconferences. Proper training on technological methods and virtual communication techniques includes attention to meeting protocol (agendas, documents, presentation slides, and handouts distributed in advance), following teleconference courtesy rules, allowing all virtual project team members adequate opportunities to speak, and keeping meetings in scope (begin and finish on time to accommodate the different time zones). A patterned, consistent method of delivering minutes, agendas, status reports, and schedule updates and a shared drive for project documentation are all part of successful virtual team communication and can help the Social Media Site Project team.

DEBRIEF FOR THE SOCIAL MEDIA SITE PROJECT CASE STUDY

In the body of knowledge for project management leadership, determining whether different leadership styles are appropriate in different situations, at different stages of the project life cycle, and with different team structures has been explored and research conducted in the project management context. The general conclusion has been that situational leadership styles can be appropriately applied to project management leadership [31]. Applying these theories and research findings provides an improved approach for managing the human resources for the Social Media Site Project. The application to human resource management is that this flexibility in leadership style can provide the Social Media Site Project with the key to profitable project work, satisfied team members, and continued organizational growth through successful virtual project deliverables. The resolution of the leadership challenges for the project manager of the Social Media Site Project involves the project manager's adopting a situational leadership style to manage and incorporate the geographically distributed team members and bringing the project to a successful completion. The project manager's current authoritarian and laissez-faire leadership styles and lack of experience and training in virtual project team management is jeopardizing the success of the Social Media Site Project. Human resource management includes productivity improvement, attracting and maintaining a skilled workforce, and organizational project management capability—all of which are threatened by the current project manager's leadership. By demonstrating a situational leadership style, the project manager can offer benefits to the organization and provide positive, successful leadership for the Social Media Site Project. This improved approach to leading and managing requires change management for all the parties involved and additional training for the project manager. The leadership challenge for the project manager to manage the geographically distributed human resources of the Social Media Site Project can be resolved by the adoption of a situational leadership style and improved virtual project management skills, enabling successful project completion.

Case Study 2.2: Too New, Too Soon

[As told by a retired, traditional project manager to the author in an interview]

OVERVIEW

I remember working once as a project manager in one very traditional, bureaucratic organization. A small (and very brave!) group in the technology area was trying a new idea called *sprints*. Interested, I investigated the new *agile* method and something called *scrum*. I talked with the individuals on the agile team, reviewed the literature, and read the original manifesto. Excited, I took the idea back to my department to give it a try.

This is not a story with a happy ending. It was way too soon for my very conservative department. The biggest problem was the team members, even the virtual team members. They were not able to change the behaviors and norms imbedded by years of being told what to do and when to do it. They were skilled, but not willing to try anything new for fear of failure and the consequences; they were taught to be responsible for only what they were told to work on; and they lacked the internal and external rewards to try anything different.

Now, years later, even the Project Management Institute has acknowledged agile as a viable methodology and offers a certification in it.

Progress!

DEBRIEF

Leadership must be shared among the team members in the agile process to be successful. The transition to agile methodology can receive resistance by traditional project managers and project team members. Most people are resistant to change and to the agile process [32], and this resistance can be difficult to overcome. Education, involvement, executive support, and a gradual move to agile can make this change more easily accepted. For information on the Project Management Institute's support of agile project management, see http://www.pmi. org/eNews/Post/2012_02-27/Agile-Minded.html. For information on the agile manifesto, see http://agilemanifesto.org/.

Case Study 2.3: It's All about Helping

[As told by an experienced virtual project manager to the author]

OVERVIEW

The definition of management is getting things done through other people, regardless of the style used. I have used other styles of management during my project management career, but not successfully. I have learned over the years that being anything other than myself in my management style risks credibility with my team and with others, especially if they get the impression that I am trying to be something both I and they know I am not. This does not mean that I am not able to be direct or make decisions for others, when I typically prefer to discuss with others impacted before making a decision; or that I cannot be unsympathetic, when I typically am a sucker for a sob story; or that I cannot be firm, when I typically try to work out a win–win situation for both sides; but there is a limit to my tolerance for any of these things. What I am referring to is trying to take on an entirely different persona in an effort to emulate a management style not compatible with my life. For me, it's all about people . . . and helping them to be better and more successful than they ever imagined being. I have always believed the mark of a good manager is their people—and you are only as good a manager as those you serve.

DEBRIEF

This project manager suggests how experience and self-confidence can help develop the most successful leadership style for an individual: "being anything other than myself in my management style risks credibility with my team and with others, especially if they get the impression that I am trying to be something both I and they know I am not." Her leadership style is closely related to servant leadership, where the servant-leader shares power and delegates, puts the needs of others first, and attempts to encourage employees to perform to their maximum potential. In this case story, we hear the project manager say, "I typically prefer to discuss with others impacted before making a decision," an indication that sharing power, delegating, and putting the needs of others first is part of her leadership style. She goes on to say, "For me, it's all about people . . . and helping them to be better and more successful than they ever imagined being," indicating that developing her team members is important to her success and the success of her project. In virtual project management, servant leadership is seen as a powerful leadership model because of the trust that is built between the project leader and team members. Her comments "being anything other than myself in my management style risks credibility" and "you are only as good a manager as those you serve" indicate a servant leadership style that is vital to her virtual leadership, one that depends upon trust, personal connections, and collaboration to be successful.

Case Study 2.4: Flexibility Is the Key

[As told by a virtual project manager to the author]

OVERVIEW

PM flexibility is a critical success factor for the virtual project's success. Flexibility is linked to the situational leadership style that says I will base my decisions on the ability and cooperation of the team members to do the job. I have to direct the new or clueless, encourage the insecure or learner through mentoring and support, and delegate everything I can to the trusted and capable high performers.

DEBRIEF

Situational leadership is a key characteristic of e-leadership [33], and situational leadership models can be used to analyze adaptive behaviors in virtual project environments [34]. Here we see the virtual project manager describing the common elements of situational leadership approaches—that the project manager (leader) should be flexible and be able to adapt and apply the appropriate model to the situation. He says, "I will base my decisions on the ability and cooperation of the team members to do the job."

Situational leadership is considered attractive for virtual project management, as it involves using different styles and allows the project manager to react to the widely changing context of project leadership [35]. Situational leadership models offer different types of leadership approaches and behaviors that can be used throughout the five project process groups: initiating, planning, executing, monitoring and controlling, and closing [36] for traditional and virtual projects. Classical situational leadership models proposed a life-cycle theory of leadership suggesting that leadership could be adjusted to the maturity and readiness of the subordinate [37]. Leadership was dependent upon workers' job maturity (task related, skills, knowledge) and psychological maturity (confidence, willingness, motivation). This provided a scale from most mature to most immature to develop four situational leadership styles dependent upon the workers' maturity: telling, selling, participating, and delegating. In this case study, we see the project manager using this scale to lead his virtual team: "I have to direct the new or clueless, encourage the insecure or learner through mentoring and support, and delegate everything I can to the trusted and capable high performers."

A situational leadership style can assist the project manager in adjusting to the maturity of the team member and in becoming more flexible in the type of leadership behavior needed, depending upon the needs of the individual. Applying existing situational leadership theories and research to nontraditional, virtual project management provides an improved approach for leading virtual projects.

FOOD FOR THOUGHT

1. What type of virtual leadership style would you suggest for an IT project? Would you suggest a different style of leadership for another type of project, such as research and development or training, for example?

2. In what scenario would you use transformational leadership with a virtual team? In what scenario would you use transactional leadership with a virtual team? Explain the differences and how you would make your decision.

3. In your own words, explain how multiple e-leadership styles can be beneficial in the virtual project management environment.

NOTES

Portions of this chapter were written by the author and are used with permission from IGI Global Publishing:

Lee, M. R. (2010). Effective virtual project management using multiple e-leadership styles. In Training Site, I. (ed.), *Encyclopedia of E-Business Development and Management in the Digital Economy: Vol. II* (445–454). Hershey, PA: IGI Global Publishing. doi:10.4018/978-1-61520-611-7.

Anonymous quotes from virtual project managers are taken from survey responses in:

Lee, M. R. (2011). *e-Leadership for project managers: A study of situational leadership and virtual project success.* ProQuest, UMI Dissertation Publishing.

Anonymous interviews:

Lee, M. R. (2013). Interviews by M. R. Lee [Tape recording.] Elkhart, IL.

REFERENCES

1. Peters, T. J., & Waterman, R. H. (1982). *In search of excellence: Lessons from America's best-run companies*. New York: Harper Collins.
2. Handy, C. (1995). Trust and the virtual organization. *Harvard Business Review*, 73, p. 40–50.
3. Spiegelman, P. (2012, November 6). The culture gap: 10 leadership practices to stop today. INC.com. Retrieved from http://www.inc.com/paul-spiegelman/leadership-practices-to-stop-today.html?goback=%252Egde_2232816_member_186153987.
4. Moorhead, G., & Griffin, R. (2004). *Organizational behavior: Managing people and organizations*. Boston: Houghton Mifflin Co.
5. Giang, V. (2012, January 27). 17 tips on becoming a charismatic leader. *Business Insider*. Retrieved from http://www.businessinsider.com/17-things-you-need-to-know-if-you-want-to-be-a-charismatic-leader-2012-1.
6. House, R. J. (1977). A 1976 theory of charismatic leadership. In Hunt, J. G. & Larson, L. L. (eds.). *Leadership: The cutting edge* (189–207). Carbondale, IL: Southern Illinois University Press.
7. Nadler, D. A., & Tushman, M. L. (1990). Beyond the charismatic leader: Leadership and organizational change. *California Management Review*, (Winter) 77–97.
8. Drucker, P. F. (1999). *Management challenges for the 21st century*. New York: Harper Collins.
9. Capella University. (2005). *Managing and organizing people*. Boston: Prentice Hall Custom Publishing.
10. Chen, M. T. (2001). Key learnings from e-project management. AACE International Transactions: Morgantown, p. IT31. Retrieved from http://www.acce.edu.au/.
11. Cascio, W. F., & Shurygailo, S. (2003). E-Leadership and virtual teams. *Organizational Dynamics*, 31(4), 362–376. doi:10.1016/S0090-2616(02)00130-4.
12. Avolio, B. J., Kahai, S., & Dodge, G. E. (2000). E-Leadership: Implications for theory, research, and practice. *Leadership Quarterly*, 11(4), 615–668. doi:10.1016/S1048-9843(00)00062-X.
13. Laufer, A. (2012). *Mastering the leadership role in project management*. Upper Saddle River, NJ: FT Press.
14. Konradt, U., & Hoch, J. E. (2007). A work roles and leadership functions of managers in virtual teams. *International Journal of e-Collaboration*, 3(2), 16–34.
15. Blanchard, K., & Blanchard, S. (2012, October 25). Why trying to manipulate employee motivation always backfires. Fast Company: Mansueto Ventures LLC. Retrieved from http://www.fastcompany.com/3002382/why-trying-manipulate-employee-motiva-tion- always-backfires?goback =%2Egde_2320211_member_190884620.
16. Hersey, P., Blanchard, K., & Johnson, D. (2001). *Management of organizational behavior: Leading human resources*. Upper Saddle River, NJ: Prentice Hall.
17. Konradt, U., & Hoch, J. E. (2007). A work roles and leadership functions of managers in virtual teams. *International Journal of E-Collaboration*, 3(2), 16–34.

18. Hertel, G., Konradt, U., & Orlikowski, B. (2004). Managing distance by interdependence: Goal setting, task interdependence and team-based rewards in virtual teams. *European Journal of Work and Organizational Psychology*, 13(1), 1–28.
19. Konradt, U., & Hoch, J. E. (2007). A work roles and leadership functions of managers in virtual teams. *International Journal of E-Collaboration*, 3(2), 16–34.
20. Hertel, G., Konradt, U., & Orlikowski, B. (2004). Managing distance by interdependence: Goal setting, task interdependence and team-based rewards in virtual teams. *European Journal of Work and Organizational Psychology*, 13(1), 1–28.
21. Hooijberg, R., & Choi, J. (2000). Which leadership roles matter to whom? An examination of rater effects on perceptions of effectiveness. *Leadership Quarterly*, 11(3), 341–364.
22. Lee-Kelley, L. (2002). Situational leadership: Managing the virtual project team. *The Journal of Management Development*, 21(5/6), 461–476.
23. Zofi, Y. S. (2011). *A manager's guide to virtual teams*. New York: AMACOM.
24. Capella University. (2005). *Managing and organizing people*. Boston: Prentice Hall Custom Publishing.
25. Hambley, L., O'Neill, T., & Kline, T. (2007). Virtual team leadership: Perspectives from the field. *International Journal of E-Collaboration*, 3(1), 40–63.
26. Kahai, S. S., & Avolio, B. J. (2008). Effects of leadership style and anonymity on arguments and intents related to acting unethically. In Kock, N. (Ed.), *E-collaboration in modern organizations: Initiating and managing distributed projects* (176–196). Hershey, PA: IGI Global Publishing.
27. Project Management Institute. (2001). *People in projects*. Newton Square, PA: Project Management Institute.
28. Kliem, R. L. (2004). *Leading high performance projects*. Boca Raton, FL: J. Ross Publishing.
29. Hambley, L., O'Neill, T., & Kline, T. (2007). Virtual team leadership: Perspectives from the field. *International Journal of E-Collaboration*, 3(1), 40–63.
30. Capella University. (2005). *Managing and organizing people*. Boston: Prentice Hall Custom Publishing.
31. Day, J. (1999). Getting the edge: The attitude of ownership. *SuperVision*, 60(6), 3–6.
32. Bell, B. S., & Kozlowski, S. W. (2002). A typology of virtual teams: Implications for effective leadership. *Group and Organization Management*, 27(1), 14–49.
33. Bell, B. S., & Kozlowski, S. W. (2002). A typology of virtual teams: Implications for effective leadership. *Group and Organization Management*, 27(1), 14–49.
34. Capella University. (2005). *Managing and organizing people*. Boston: Prentice Hall Custom Publishing.
35. Wickham, K. R., & Walther, J. B. (2007). Perceived behaviors of emergent and assigned leaders in virtual groups. *International Journal of E-Collaboration*, 3(1), 1–17.
36. Fiedler, F. E. (1967). *A theory of leadership effectiveness*. New York: McGraw-Hill.
37. Kliem, R. L. (2004). *Leading high performance projects*. Boca Raton, FL: J. Ross Publishing.
38. Fiedler, F. E. (1967). *A theory of leadership effectiveness*. New York: McGraw-Hill.
39. Tannebaum, R., & Schmidt, W. H. (1958). How to choose a leadership pattern. *Harvard Business Review*, 36(2), 95–101.
40. Hersey, P., & Blanchard, K. (1969). Life cycle theory of leadership. *Training and Development Journal*, 23(5), 26–34.
41. Vroom, V. (2000). Leadership and the decision-making process. *Organizational Dynamics*, 28(4), 82–94.

42. Slevin, D. P., & Pinto, J. K. (1991). Project leadership: Understanding and consciously choosing your style. *Project Management Journal*, 12(1), 39–47.

43. Serena. (2007). An introduction to agile software development. Retrieved from http://www.cs.utexas.edu/users/downing/papers/Agile2007.pdf.

44. Illyas, N. (2011). Agile project management methodologies: A practical approach. Ed Ventures E-Learning. Retrieved May 16, 2012, from focus.com.

45. Cohn, M. (2011). What is scrum? Agile software development and scrum. Retrieved from http://www.mountaingoatsoftware.com/topics/scrum.

46. Cohn, M. (2011). What is scrum? Agile software development and scrum. Retrieved from http://www.mountaingoatsoftware.com/topics/scrum.

47. Highsmith, J. (2004). *Agile project management: Creating innovative products*. Boston: Pearson Education Inc.

48. Humphrey, W. S., & Booch, G. (October 2010). Agile methods, open source, and cloud computing. Pearson InformIT. Retrieved from http://www.informit.com/articles/article.aspx?p = 1644836.

49. Highsmith, J. (2004). *Agile project management: Creating innovative products*. Boston: Pearson Education Inc.

50. Lucas, K. A. (2007). Examining servant leadership within virtual and face-to-face teams. *Dissertation Abstracts International*, 68/11, suppl. A, 105 p.

51. Lemenager, E. (2009). Virtual servant leadership. Elliottlemenager. Retrieved from http://www.elliottlemenager.com/2009/01/07/virtual-servant-leadership/.

52. Lemenager, E. (2009). Virtual servant leadership. Elliottlemenager. Retrieved from http://www.elliottlemenager.com/2009/01/07/virtual-servant-leadership/.

53. Umlas, J. W. (2012). *Grateful leadership: Using the power of acknowledgment to engage all your people and achieve superior results*. New York: McGraw-Hill.

54. Tuckman, B. (1965). Developmental sequence in small groups. *Psychological Bulletin*, 63, 384–399.

55. Duarte, D., & Snyder, N. (1999). *Mastering virtual teams*. San Francisco: Jossey-Bass.

56. Keller, J. M. (2008). An integrative theory of motivation, volition, and performance. *Technology, Instruction, Cognition, and Learning*, 6, 79–104.

57. Mayer, M. (2010). *The virtual edge: Embracing technology for distributed project team success*. Atlanta: Project Management Institute, Inc.

58. Pinchot, G. 1985. *Intrapreneuring: Why you don't have to leave the corporation to become an entrepreneur*. New York: Harper & Row.

59. Fernald, L. W. Jr., Solomon, G. T., & Tarabishy, A. (2005). A new paradigm: Entrepreneurial leadership. *Southern Business Review*, 30(2), 1–10.

60. Anonymous. (2012). Effective team building for stronger teams. Trytop.com. Retrieved from http://articles.trytop.com/team-building/Effective-Team-Building-for-Stronger-Teams_45403/.

61. Lesonsky, R. (2012). The freelance economy: Is this the future of work? *Business on Main*. Retrieved from http://businessonmain.msn.com/browseresources/articles/smallbusinesstrends.aspx?cp-documentid=30876276&wt.mc_id=linkedin&goback=%2Egde_2320211_member_198162575#fbid=CNmqG6QfEdQ.

62. Garey, P. (2007). The agility factor: Key characteristics of the highly agile professional. Extreme Agility. www.extremeagility.com. Retrieved from http://www.ipacweb.org/conf/07/garey.pdf.

63. Clegg, E., & Quinn, C. N. (2004/2009). The agility factor. In Conner, M. L., & Clawson, J. G. (eds.), *Creating a learning culture: Strategy, technology and practice* (208–223). Cambridge, MA: Cambridge University Press.

64. Garey, P. (2007). The agility factor: Key characteristics of the highly agile professional. Extreme Agility. www.extremeagility.com. Retrieved from http://www.ipacweb.org/conf/07/garey.pdf.

65. Garey, P. (2007). The agility factor: Key characteristics of the highly agile professional. Extreme Agility. www.extremeagility.com. Retrieved from http://www.ipacweb.org/conf/07/garey.pdf.

66. London, M. (2001). *Leadership development: Paths to self-insight and professional growth*. Mahwah, NJ: Lawrence Erlbaum Associates.

67. Garton, C., & Wegryn, K. (2006). *Managing without walls*. Lewisville, TX: Mc Press Online, LP.

68. Podsakoff, P. M., & Scheiesheim, C. (1985). Field studies of French and Raven's bases of power: Critique, reanalysis, and suggestions for future research. *Psychological Bulletin*, 97(3), 387–411.

69. English, L. (2004). The 7 habits of highly effective information professionals. *DM Review*, 24(8), 38–65.

70. Kliem, R. L. (2004). *Leading high performance projects*. Boca Raton, FL: J. Ross Publishing.

71. Verma, V. K. (1997). *Managing the project team*. Newtown Square, PA: Project Management Institute.

72. Pinto, J. K., Thoms, P., Trailer, J., Palmer, T., & Govekar, M. (1998). *Project leadership from theory to practice*. Newtown Square, PA: Project Management Institute.

73. Dauten, D. (1999). *The gifted boss: How to find, create and keep great employees*. New York: William Morrow and Company, Inc.

74. Project Management Institute. (2001). *People in projects*. Newtown Square, PA: Project Management Institute.

75. Podsakoff, P. M., & Scheiesheim, C. (1985). Field studies of French and Raven's bases of power: Critique, reanalysis, and suggestions for future research. *Psychological Bulletin*, 97(3), 387–411.

76. Skogstad, A., Einarsen, S., Torsheim, T., Aasland, M. S., & Hetland, H. (2007). The destructiveness of laissez-faire leadership behavior. *Journal of Occupational Health & Psychology*, 12(1), 80–92.

77. Mindtools. (2013). The leader-member exchange theory: Getting the best from all team members. Mindtools. Retrieved from http://www.mindtools.com/pages/article/leader-member-exchange.htm.

78. Dansereau, F., Graen, G., & Hgag, W. J. (1975). A vertical dyad linkage approach to leadership within formal organizations: A longitudinal investigation of the role-making process. *Organizational Behavior and Human Performance*, 15, 46–78.

79. Whipple, R. (2013). Favoritism is a huge problem. Leadergrow, Inc. Retrieved from http://leadergrow.com/articles/43-favoritism-is-a-huge-problem.

80. Wiener, N. (1950). *The human use of human beings*. New York: Anchor Books.

81. Mayer, M. (2010). *The virtual edge: Embracing technology for distributed project team success*. Atlanta: Project Management Institute, Inc.

82. Turner, J. R., & Muller, R. (2005). The project manager's leadership style as a success factor on projects: A literature review. *Project Management Journal*, 36(2), 49–61.

83. Turner, J. R., & Muller, R. (2005). The project manager's leadership style as a success factor on projects: A literature review. *Project Management Journal*, 36(2), 49–61.

84. Baldoni, J. (2012, December 4). What's your leadership style: Woof-woof or wag-wag? *Forbes*. Retrieved from http://www.forbes.com/sites/johnbaldoni/2012/12/04/whats-your-leadership-style-woof-woof-or-wag-wag/?goback =%2Egde_2648175_.

85. Pauleen, D. J. (2003). Leadership in a global virtual team: An action learning approach. *Leadership & Organization Development Journal*, 24(3), 153–162. doi: 10.1108/01437730310469570.
86. Pauleen, D. J. (2003). Leadership in a global virtual team: An action learning approach. *Leadership & Organization Development Journal*, 24(3), 153–162. doi: 10.1108/01437730310469570.

CASE STUDY REFERENCES

1. Nelson, D. L., & Quick, J. C. (1996). *Organizational behavior: The essentials*. St. Paul, MN: West Publishing Company.
2. Moorhead, G., & Griffin, R. (2004). *Organizational behavior: Managing people and organizations*. Boston: Houghton Mifflin Co.
3. Handy, C. (1993). *Understanding organizations*. New York: Oxford University Press.
4. Mitchell, T. R., Holtom, B. C., & Lee, T. W. (2001). How to keep your best employees: Developing an effective retention policy—Executive commentary. *The Academy of Management Executive*, 15(4), 96–109.
5. Mayfield, J., & Mayfield, M. (2008). The creative environment's influence on intent to turnover: A structural equation model and analysis. *Management Research News*, 31(1), 41–56.
6. Bhatnagar, J. (2007). Talent management strategy of employee engagement in Indian ITES employees: Key to retention. *Employee Relations*, 29(6), 640–663.
7. Kendra, K., & Taplin, L. J. (2004). Project success: A cultural framework. *Project Management Journal*, 35(1), 30–45.
8. Lan-Ying, D., & Yong-Dong, S. (2007). Implement business strategy via project portfolio management: A model and case study. *Journal of American Academy of Business*, 11(2), 239–244.
9. Srivannaboon, S. (2006). Linking project management with business strategy. *Project Management Journal*, 37(5), 88–96.
10. London, M. (2001). *Leadership development: Paths to self-insight and professional growth*. Mahwah, NJ: Lawrence Erlbaum Associates.
11. Lee-Kelley, L. (2002). Situational leadership: Managing the virtual project team. *The Journal of Management Development*, 21(5/6), 461–476.
12. Konradt, U., & Hoch, J. E. (2007). A work roles and leadership functions of managers in virtual teams. *International Journal of E-Collaboration*, 3(2), 16–34.
13. Wickham, K. R., & Walther, J. B. (2007). Perceived behaviors of emergent and assigned leaders in virtual groups. *International Journal of E-Collaboration*, 3(1), 1–17.
14. Vroom, V. H., & Jago, A. G. (2007). The role of the situation in leadership. *American Psychologist*, 62(1), 17–24.
15. Dansereau, F., Graen, G., & Hgag, W. J. (1975). A vertical dyad linkage approach to leadership within formal organizations: A longitudinal investigation of the role-making process. *Organizational Behavior and Human Performance*, 15, 46–78.
16. Project Management Institute. (2004). *A guide to the project management body of knowledge: PMBOK® guide* (3rd ed.). Newton Square, PA: Project Management Institute.

17. Joshi, K. (1991). A model of users' perspective on change: The case of information systems technology implementation. *MIS Quarterly,* 15(2), 229–242.

18. Christensen, C., Marx, M., & Stevenson, H. (2006). The tools of cooperation and change. *Harvard Business Review,* 84(10), 73–80.

19. Verma, V. K. (1997). *Managing the project team.* Newton Square, PA: Project Management Institute.

20. Christensen, C., Marx, M., & Stevenson, H. (2006). The tools of cooperation and change. *Harvard Business Review,* 84(10), 73–80.

21. Verma, V. K. (1997). *Managing the project team.* Newton Square, PA: Project Management Institute.

22. Kliem, R. L. (2004). *Leading high performance projects.* Boca Raton, FL: J. Ross Publishing.

23. Kerzner, H. (2006). *Project management: A systems approach to planning, scheduling, and controlling.* Hoboken, NJ: John Wiley & Sons, Inc.

24. Goman, C. K. (2004). *This isn't the company I joined: How to lead in business turned upside down.* Berkley, CA: KCS Publishing.

25. London, M. (2001). *Leadership development: Paths to self-insight and professional growth.* Mahwah, NJ: Lawrence Erlbaum Associates.

26. Altemeyer, B. (1999). To thine own self be untrue: Self-awareness in authoritarians. *North American Journal of Psychology,* 1(2), 157–165.

27. Tannebaum, R., & Schmidt, W. H. (1958). How to choose a leadership pattern. *Harvard Business Review,* 36(2), 95–101.

28. Hersey, P., & Blanchard, K. (1969). Life cycle theory of leadership. *Training and Development Journal,* 23(5), 26–34.

29. Vroom, V. H., & Jago, A. G. (2007). The role of the situation in leadership. *American Psychologist,* 62(1), 17–24.

30. Haywood, M. (1998). *Managing virtual teams: Practical techniques for high-technology project managers.* Boston: Artech House.

31. Turner, J. R., & Muller, R. (2005). The project manager's leadership style as a success factor on projects: A literature review. *Project Management Journal,* 36(2), 49–61.

32. Vin. (2012). Resistance to agile development is not inevitable. *Brainslink.com.* Retrieved from http://brainslink.com/2012/03/resistance-to-agile-development-is-not-inevitable/.

33. Day, J., & Bobeva, M. (2003, December). Successful IS project leaders: A situational theory perspective. *Electronic Journal of Information Systems Evaluation (EJISE),* 6(2), Paper 9. Retrieved from http://www.ejise.com/index.htm.

34. Pulley, M. L., & Sessa, V. I. (2001). e-Leadership: Tackling complex challenges. *Industrial and Commercial Training,* 33(6/7), 225–229. doi:10.1108/00197850110405379.

35. Prabhakar, G. P. (2006). A switch in time saves nine: Discovering a new methodology to succeed in projects using transformational leadership in cross-cultural settings. *Dissertation Abstracts International,* 67(01), 262. (UMI No. 1126786541).

36. Project Management Institute. (2013). *A guide to the project management body of knowledge: PMBOK® guide* (5th ed.). Newton Square, PA: Project Management Institute.

37. Hersey, P., & Blanchard, K. (1969). Life cycle theory of leadership. *Training and Development Journal,* 23(5), 26–34.

3

Enhancing Virtual Project Communications

The phrase "What we've got here is failure to communicate," made famous by the 1967 movie *Cool Hand Luke*, could apply to many virtual projects. Communication training and skills are essential for the leaders in any organization—traditional, hybrid, or virtual. In a recent survey of business leaders, 97% responded that good communication skills were important for being an effective leader in the digital economy [1]. An understanding of technology, the nuances of virtual communication, the advantages of periodic face-to-face communication, collaboration tools, and media are all part of the communications competencies necessary for e-leaders. Providing value to the organization for successful virtual project leadership through good communications is, and will continue to be, essential in the nontraditional work environment of the 21st century.

Cultural sensitivity is such an important issue in virtual communications—enough to warrant a separate discussion of unique cultural communication techniques for the e-leader—that it is covered in Chapter 4 of this book.

UNDERSTANDING PROJECT COMMUNICATIONS

Many project managers will describe the best communication practices for any type of project management as the three C's: Communicate, communicate, communicate. Communication is the basis for all human interaction and is a vital and essential skill. The basic communication model remains constant for all types of communication—there must be a sender, a message, a medium used to communicate, and a receiver. Generally communication is sender controlled, but in virtual communications the communication is usually receiver controlled [2]. The receiver can choose to respond to the e-mail, voice mail, text, tweet, or other communication, unlike in face-to-face communication, which requires immediate response and feedback. This lag time in response can cause the sender to wonder if the message was received, increase misinterpretation of the communication process, and permit the receiver to control the timing of the response to the sender—all of which compound the frequency and seriousness of miscommunication and communication errors. The impact of the miscommunication or errors may not show up for months, making it essential that the project manager understand and be trained in virtual communication tools and techniques.

e-Leadership for Virtual Project Communications

e-Leaders working in a distributed project environment need to be excellent communicators and have the ability to overcome the challenges involved with virtual communications. Their goal should be to keep all stakeholders and team members engaged, regardless of location, and effectively communicate to all individuals involved in the project. Challenges in communication can lead to difficulties in task completion and productivity in the project. Communication is essential to the success of projects and closely related to performance and productivity. Research suggests that virtuality influences include shared understanding, which may in turn influence productivity [3]. The project manager has the responsibility of explicitly communicating the focus and function for each team member, rather than assuming that it is understood.

Planning for Project Communications

Regardless of the methodology used for the project, the project manager is responsible for ensuring that the organization, stakeholders, and team remain informed throughout the project life cycles. To be successful in obtaining the goal of a fully functioning virtual team, the project manager needs to have additional training in virtual communication skills. The communication competency is involved in all five project management process groups (initiating, planning, executing, monitoring and controlling, and closing) and is an essential skill for successful project managers [4]. The project manager should analyze the following project inputs when developing the communications plan with the team—communication requirements, communication technology, communication models, and communication methods [5]. The development of the project's communications plan should be a team effort, not solely an activity performed by the project manager. When projects are similar, the project manager can present a communications plan from a similar project as a template for the new project, but communications plans should not be blindly copied from one project to the next. The team should thoroughly review the following:

- Messages that need to be conveyed
- Frequency of the communications
- Outcome of the communications
- Audience(s) for each message
- Level of detail needed for each audience and message
- Best format for each audience and message [6]

The importance of thorough communication planning ensures that good communication will happen, when it will happen, who will be communicated with and how, as well as transparency for the project. For the majority of project managers, this is detailed in the project's communications plan. The project manager and team should set ground rules regarding expectations for returning phone messages, reading and answering e-mails, and posting messages. During the early phases of the project, these guidelines should be detailed in the team's project charter. A good flow of communication to and from the virtual team can build trust within the team, eliminate feelings of isolation for some team members, improve decision making by providing clear and important information quickly, and more quickly move the project toward success.

Communications Plan

The traditional project management communications plan can be used to present patterned, consistent, standardized procedures and processes to facilitate positive virtual communications. However, increased communication does not necessarily mean better collaboration in virtual teams. In an empirical analysis of virtual teams' communication patterns, Sarker and Sahay [7] clarified how communication, virtual team development, and collaboration were related. They encourage communications planning as the foundation for the best possible virtual communication management. Proactive sharing of information, monitoring and managing electronic communication, facilitating team meetings, and ensuring that team members have enough information to be successful are the responsibilities of leadership [8]. A patterned, consistent method of delivering minutes, agendas, status reports, and schedule updates and a shared drive for project documentation are all part of successful virtual team communication. To ensure that this occurs and that communications are clear, a communications plan is essential for effective management of both traditional and virtual projects.

An effective communications plan is, therefore, critical. The team compiles the communications plan during the planning phase, or individuals with experience and expertise in communications can draft the plan for the review and approval. The communications plan includes the type of communication, purpose of the communication, owner, audience, frequency of the communication, and documentation procedures in a chart-type format. An audience analysis, including an analysis of the most appropriate method by which to communicate, is necessary for all stakeholders, ensuring that they are receiving the correct information at the correct time in the program. The communications plan may be prepared in a format that can be sorted (such as Excel), but the plan can also be done in any software, such as a Word document. The communication planning process [9] can help determine the best way to communicate with stakeholders at all levels and the correct method(s) of communication distribution. Project communication management includes not only the distribution of communication messages but also the compilation and storage of program information. Because most of the project manager's time is spent communicating, a project communications plan is vital to the success of the project.

Table 3.1 provides an example of a simple communications plan for a project with an online training class as the deliverable.

Several types of general project communication are required and need to be documented throughout the project life cycle. Some common types of communication are shown in Table 3.2.

TABLE 3.1

Sample Communications Plan

Communications Plan: Online Training Project

Core Message Points: This training will provide instruction for the sales force to be able to enter new sales in 10 minutes or less with 99% accuracy using the new online technology to enhance the customer service satisfaction rating by 45% over the next three years.

Internal to Project

To	From	Timing	Communication Objective
Core Team	Project Manager	Weekly	Project team progress meeting agendas
Sponsors	Project Manager	Weekly	Update sponsors on project team activities and escalate any issues needing resolution
Project Team	Project Manager	Weekly	Update work plan, project status
Core Team	Team (shared)	Weekly	Meeting minutes—recap of meeting discussion around agenda items
Core Team	Project Manager	Weekly	Project schedule awareness—project timeline and due dates surrounding project work, project status report
Project Team	Project Manager	As needed	Update project plan
Core Team	Project Manager	As needed	Issue log updates—issues needing escalation or immediate attention
Sponsors, Key Stakeholders	Project Manager	Monthly	Project status report—list of accomplishments over the past month, expected accomplishments over the next 2–4 weeks, and outstanding issues and proposed solutions
Stakeholders	Project Manager	Quarterly	Project status report—update stakeholders on project team activities
Executive Sponsor	Project Manager	Once	Final formal report

(continued)

TABLE 3.1

Sample Communications Plan (continued)

External to Project

Phases: A = Analysis Phase, D = Design Phase, Dev = Development Phase, I = Implementation Phase, E = Evaluation Phase [10]

To	From	Phase	Communication Objective
Executive Sales Manager(s)	Project Manager	A	Core message points, communications plan
Key Stakeholders	Executive Sales Manager(s)	D	Build awareness, establish business need Consider including an example of importance and need for training
Various, including Subject Matter Experts (SMEs), Stakeholders, Sponsors	Project Team	Dev	Showcase project deliverables using a presentation platform; focus on "quick wins" and development progress
Managers	Executive Sales Manager(s)	Dev	Inform managers of new training, plans for launch, and ask for any suggestions around support
Assistant Managers	Managers	Dev	Inform assistant managers of new training, plans for launch, and ask for any suggestions around support
Key Stakeholders	Executive Sales Manager(s)	I	Announce training available
Managers, Assistant Managers	Communications Team	I	Announce training when available with suggested communication around completion expectations
Organization—General Sales Departments	Communications Team	I	Announcement memo—training available and the benefits of completing the training
Organization—General Sales Departments	Communications Team	I	Article/Reminder—benefits of the training, completion expectations
Executive Sales Manager(s)	Assessments Team	E	Initial effectiveness of training
Key Stakeholders	Executive Sales Manager(s)	E	Initial effectiveness of training
Various, including SMEs, Stakeholders, Sponsors	Assessments Team	E	Training Evaluation—collecting data and measuring the transfer of learning on the job

TABLE 3.2

Common Types of Project Communication

Type of Communication	Purpose of Communication	Owner	Audience	Frequency	Documentation
Project Status Meeting	Update work plan, issue resolution, project status	Project Manager	Project Team	Weekly	Meeting Minutes
Issues Log	Issue monitoring	Project Manager and Project Team	Project Team	Ongoing	Issues Log Database
Ongoing Project Status	Show project schedule/status as a whole	Project Manager or Team Lead	Project Team	As needed	Report
Formal Project Status	Show project status as a whole	Project Manager/ Team Lead	Stakeholders, Sponsors, Steering Committee	Every 3 weeks or as determined in communications plan	Report
Stakeholders– Sponsors Project Status Meeting	Establish if project is on track and is meeting expectations	Project Manager	Stakeholders, Project Sponsors, Project Team	Every 4 weeks or as determined in communications plan	Report for Stakeholders/ Sponsors
Lessons Learned	Evaluate the project	Project Manager or Mediator	Project Team	At the end of each project phase, or at the halfway point of the project and at the end of the project	Lessons Learned Database

VARIOUS APPROACHES TO VIRTUAL COMMUNICATION

Different Methods

Assuming that one particular communication medium works for all communications is a common pitfall for virtual management [11]. The e-leader and team should assess voice mail, blogs, wikis, teleconferences, fax, e-mail, videoconferences, electronic bulletin or discussion boards, collaboration sites, and other media in the early stages of the project to determine the most effective methods or tools for communication for the project and the team. The best methods are the ones that all team members have equal and immediate access to and are trained on, and are effective for everyone.

Categorizing communication media into synchronous and asynchronous tools and the number of participants necessary is helpful in organizing virtual communications [12]. *Synchronous* tools include face-to-face meetings (not virtual), video- or teleconferencing, screen sharing, chat rooms, and chat or instant messaging. Chat or instant messaging allows very short, synchronous, typewritten "talk" where questions can be asked and responses can be made quickly. Videoconferencing allows people to see and hear one another in real time in a one-on-one or team setting. *Asynchronous* tools include voice mail, e-mail, fax, postal mail, team rooms, websites, collaboration sites, bulletin boards, text, and blogs or discussion groups. These tools do not allow for real-time communication. Figures 3.1

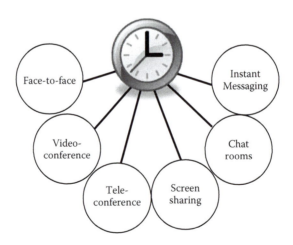

FIGURE 3.1
Synchronous tools.

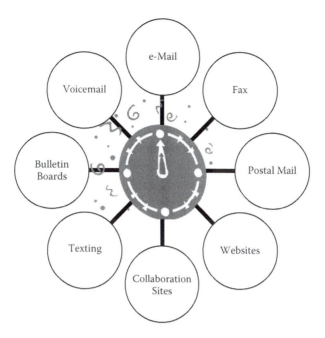

FIGURE 3.2
Asynchronous tools.

and 3.2 show how some of these tools can be organized as synchronous (same time and place or same time but different place) or asynchronous (different time and different place).

This categorization strategy allows the correct communication tools to be implemented into the communications plan to facilitate the team's information sharing.

Tools and Techniques to Enhance Communications for Virtual Organizations

Tools and techniques to enhance communications for virtual organizations should be an integration of both traditional and virtual methodologies, processes, and theories. Applying proven traditional project management practices with updated modification and focused training can provide an effective road map for success. To improve communications, the organization should establish a common ground for communication and use networking within the organization to create information sharing.

Communications Technology

The virtual team relies upon technology to communicate, such as e-mail, voicemail, teleconferences, and videoconferences. Proper training on technological methods and virtual communication techniques includes attention to meeting protocol (agendas, documents, presentation slides, and handouts distributed in advance), following teleconference courtesy rules, allowing all virtual team members adequate opportunities to speak, and keeping meetings in scope (begin and finish on time to accommodate different time zones). Both the teleconference and videoconference should not last more than two hours and both require good preparation to keep the team engaged in the conversation. Case in point—one virtual worker shared the story that she would take a bath, read the newspaper, and clean house during team meetings!

Traditional and newer software tools abound for the 21st century e-leader to use for effective communication. The most advanced technologies, such as Microsoft's Lync, integrate multiple communication channels in a cloud-based platform that includes e-mail; voice over Internet protocol (VoIP); instant messaging; audio-, video-, and web-conferencing; chat; and DeskShare services. Table 3.3 suggests some of the more common tools.

The type of communication should be matched to the type of message being communicated. Table 3.4 gives several examples of the communication need or problem and the most effective communication tool to use for managing the need or problem [13].

e-Mail is one of the most common forms of communication in virtual projects, and is a multipurpose tool that can be used to share thoughts to documents. Because e-mail is not real time, it allows the receiver the

TABLE 3.3

Communication Need and Example Software Tools

Communication Need	Example Software Tools
Document management	E-room, Google Docs, Steelray, MS EPM
Collaborative, cloud, or company databases	Sharepoint, Google Docs
Scheduling	MS Project Server, Quick Arrow, Spotlight
Instant messaging	IM, Short Messaging Service SMS
Videoconferencing	Google Gang, NetMeeting, Lync
Virtual meetings	MS NetMeeting, Webex, MS Live Meeting
Phone conferencing	GoToMeeting, ChatStage, Lync
e-Mail	Microsoft Outlook, Gmail
Tracking and reporting	TeamIntel, SureTrak, Projectplace

TABLE 3.4

Communication Need/Problem and Most Effective Tool

Communication Need/Problem	Most Effective Tool
Long e-mail chains	Phone call
Bad news or personal information, performance problems, initial planning	Face-to-face
Sensitive or confidential information	Phone call or face-to-face
Reports, meeting notes	Collaboration database
Positive team milestone news or updates	Social media or conference call
Individual kudos	Phone call, face-to-face, or personal e-mail
Team kudos	Collaboration database, e-mail

control to carefully compose a reply before sending it. It is also one of the most "dangerous" forms of virtual communication. Do not use e-mail—

- in a confidential situation
- to deliver bad or sensitive news
- if there is a chance you might be misunderstood
- if you need an immediate response
- if privacy is an issue
- for detailed, in-depth information or instructions
- to debate a topic

It is important to remember that e-mail, like personal chatting at the water cooler, should not be just all business. Use e-mail as an avenue to encourage interpersonal communication by adding a personal touch that reflects an understanding of the receiver's background, interests, or home life. Writing e-mails to team members using a personal tone, similar to what would be used when speaking to someone in person, is more effective than a formal, impersonal tone. Like other electronic communications, anyone who receives an e-mail also has the Forward and Print options. It is impossible to take back what has been written once the Send button has been pushed. e-Mail communications are considered "in writing," making documentation easier, and are also considered discoverable evidence for lawsuits.

Virtual Etiquette

Communications for virtual teams requires sensitivity to language, particularly tone, style, sociolinguistic variations, and use of slang [14]. The organization can assist the team by providing this training, including cross-cultural understanding (including time zones), e-etiquette, and establishing commonalities, in addition to training on various electronic communication technologies. Leadership should always set a good example and privately coach any individual whose communications style might be difficult for others in the virtual organization.

Sharing Knowledge

e-Leaders need to be extremely organized to be able to monitor work in remote locations. This requires the ability to get information as well as give information to the virtual team. Feedback and acknowledgment of shared knowledge is vital to the success of the project. Acknowledgments can be required through electronic response mechanisms, and feedback should be encouraged with processes in place to facilitate both positive and negative feedback within the virtual team. Talking through requirements, test cases, strategy, and review procedures are important in the virtual environment. This will require additional time, and the project manager should allocate extra time compared with face-to-face communication. With members who require more structure, e-leaders need to spend more time detailing the task. With members who require less structure, detailing the task will cause them to feel micromanaged [15]. When providing confirmation of decisions, the virtual manager should follow up in writing. Meeting minutes should be completed and dispersed as soon as possible and should include the opportunity for team members to edit or correct the minutes within a stated timeline.

Communicating in a Nonverbal World

Many of the nonverbal communications that collocated teams take for granted are not available to the virtual team. Nonverbal cues are missing in the virtual world. Body language is 55% of communication, words comprise only 7% of communication—but tone and inflection are considered 38% [16]. Norms and unwritten rules, voice tonality and inflection, facial expressions, body language, social interaction, and gestures are some of the missing elements of communication for virtual team members [17]. Gestures can be easily misinterpreted in face-to-face international and multicultural communications. This is one area of communications the project manager of the virtual team does not have to be concerned about when facilitating teleconferences or e-mail threads. The traditional, collocated team has the advantage of being able to see and hear oral conversations; often the virtual team has the ability to only hear or read. Without the benefit of face-to-face interaction and physical cues, team members can misinterpret the meaning of communications.

Misinterpretation of written communication can also be damaging to the virtual team, which is due to the inability to identify nonverbal cues. Certain rules of etiquette have evolved for electronic written communications:

- Do not send e-mails to everyone if only a few people need to know the information. And do not send junk mail or chain letters.
- Angry, offensive, or insulting messages have no place in the business environment, and especially not in electronic communications.
- Shouting is not allowed in the traditional workplace. Using CAPITAL LETTERS in the virtual environment is the equivalent to shouting out loud. Use upper- and lowercase sentence style.
- Watch the use of acronyms, abbreviations, and jargon.
- If a document or a link is attached, be sure it is active.
- Smileys and emoticons (electronic symbols of emotions such as :->) should be avoided in business writing.
- Follow the "no-scrolling" rule and keep e-mails concise, short, and to the point.

The *subject* line is the first impression in virtual communication. Subject lines should be descriptive and complete. Many readers prioritize their in-box by looking at the subject line. The subject line "Meeting" is not as effective as "Team Meeting – 8 a.m. – 2/27."

The *body* of the communication should be easy to read. Paragraphs should be simple and contain only one idea. A blank line between paragraphs will make your communication easier to read. Bulleted lists can help summarize main points and numbered lists can help your reader put things in order. White space will increase readability.

The *closing* is often omitted in electronic communication. However, it may add a friendly and personalized touch. Action items or reminder lines, such as "We'll have a teleconference on Friday morning at 8:00," are frequently used to close and remind the reader of any important information contained in the body.

The reader has only written words to understand the message when gestures and facial expressions are not available. Team members are usually busy, and communications need to be clear and concise. Particular

TABLE 3.5

Communication Tips

✓	**Communication Tips**
☐	Limit communications to one subject. If a message is longer than one screen (one page) or has several ideas included in it, your reader will probably not read it. Split long communications into shorter ones, and stay with one main topic for each.
☐	Be concise. For example, write, "Chris, I'm attaching the information you need," instead of "In our team meeting last month, someone brought up the point that you needed additional information about the new products."
☐	Be specific. "Please make 20 copies of the product report by tomorrow afternoon" is better wording than "As per our conversation, please make copies of the report as requested as soon as possible."
☐	Use headings, such as Summary, Action Needed, or Recommendations, to help the team member follow your thoughts.
☐	Use active voice and present tense: "He is extending the deadline" is better than "He said the project deadline has been extended." And "We are not satisfied with the approval rating" is better than "We were not satisfied with the approval rating."
☐	Avoid negative words like *no, not, don't, can't*, and *never*. Use positive words, and don't forget *please* and *thank you*.
☐	Keep your messages simple. Use short words, sentences, and paragraphs. Sentences more than 8–15 words or longer than two typed lines should be broken into two sentences. A paragraph should be no longer than six typed lines.
☐	Compose your messages offline. Proofread your messages and use a word processing system to help check your spelling. Save a draft for review later, then send the information.

attention should be given to tone—and proofreading is a must. The checklist in Table 3.5 can be helpful for the virtual communicator.

It is strongly suggested that smiling when in teleconferences can be an effective technique to encourage communication [18]. As the late comedian Phyllis Diller would say, "A smile is the curve that sets everything straight."

Jokes and comical comments can be misinterpreted in the virtual world. If a team member is making a joke, it is recommended that the project manager say: "The people on the phone cannot see that John is smiling, but I'll bet he is" [19]. Humor is healthy, but in the virtual world it often needs clarification.

Best Practice Approaches

Face-to-Face Communications

Face-to-face meetings or videoconferencing are considered the best tools to be used during the planning phase of the project. When done early in the project, team members have an opportunity to learn about each other, discuss how they like to communicate, and build relationships that enable them to work together better [20]. After the scoping and initiation phase of the project is completed, it is recommended that the project manager host a traditional kickoff meeting for virtual projects that brings all virtual members together face-to-face. At the kickoff meeting project team members should establish good relationships with each other and the project manager, which will enhance virtual communication and productivity later in the project [21]. A face-to-face kickoff meeting can enhance ongoing electronic communications, help identify and resolve issues, and set a common understanding [22]. An initial videoconference meeting can reap similar benefits if a face-to-face meeting is not possible. According to Weisenfeld, "There is evidence that when people have even just one face-to-face meeting, it makes virtual teams work much more smoothly" [23]. Many seasoned virtual project managers will attest that, if possible, spending time knowing the team members at the early stage of the project and introducing face-to-face communications at key milestones makes a difference to the success of the project. One project manager suggests: "Do more face-to-face communication... it will help both parties. Draw the picture instead of describing it to a blindfolded team. Use video-enabled collaboration tools" (anonymous). It is suggested that the team meet at least once face-to-face. If possible, assemble your team for the kickoff meeting and, if it is an extended project, at least once a year [24]. Face-to-face and videoconferencing tools can build trust and understanding by providing the ability for the virtual team to hear and see each other in real time.

Teleconferences and Telephone Calls

Teleconferences and telephone calls provide one-on-one or group real-time communication that allows for clarification and discussion, idea sharing, and decision making [25]. Driskell, Radtke, and Salas [26] strongly suggest the use of audio over text-based communications. However, other studies do not confirm the advantages of group problem solving or better outcomes using audio combined with video as a medium for communications. Several studies have found that video communications do not enhance the virtual communications efforts [27]. The use of teleconferencing depends upon the nature and needs of the team. Teleconferences, similar to other meetings, require an agenda and purpose to be productive. Handouts and presentation slides should be made available to virtual team members well ahead of the meeting if the team is a hybrid team. As the e-leader of the call, it is important to recognize new members and make time for social discourse prior to the beginning of the meeting. Some virtual project managers allow five minutes at the beginning of each teleconference for "visiting" and social conversation. A regular routine for teleconference meetings will allow for team members to feel comfortable and encourage conversation, ending the reputation of poor teleconferencing as "it's too long and nothing important happened."

Often forgotten in virtual communication discussions, but no less important, is the use of a simple telephone call from the project manager to the team member. Calling each team member personally is a strong indicator of good communication skills for the virtual project manager. The connection of person-to-person voice communication often gives clues regarding the emotional indicators and can help disseminate complex information. The relationship building from personal phone calls can reap benefits in productivity and employee engagement. e-Mails can build up a communication barrier, so whenever possible the e-leader should try to break the e-mail pattern with a video chat or telephone call.

Collaboration Tools

The purpose of collaboration sites is that documents can be shared, modified, stored, and retrieved with easy access in one location. Providing a site for documentation improves openness and transparency within the project team. Collaboration tools should be selected based on the phase of the project [28]. The selection of the appropriate and effective communications media is therefore dependent upon the needs of the team and the personalities of the team members. Cloud computing continues to grow, and mobile apps may soon provide team members and e-leaders a new venue for leveraging data faster and more easily. Organizations that are able to tie multiple electronic systems together will provide employees with ways to access information and assimilate data faster. These advantages will allow the virtual project manager the ability to help the organization maintain a competitive advantage, leveraging the wisdom of the team rather than just the management.

Social media is an option for virtual project communication. Many projects have "gone social." According to Khan [29]: "When you consider the many new social collaboration and social networking tools now available to help professionals and businesses communicate and collaborate with their peers more efficiently, it's mind-boggling to think many people in the enterprise still get weighed down with the daily confines of e-mail." The disadvantages of e-mail are becoming increasingly evident, as seen in Figure 3.3.

e-Mail		Social Collaboration and Networking	
Advantages	**Disadvantages**	**Advantages**	**Disadvantages**
Personalized messages	Full e-mail in-boxes, inability to keep up with multiple messages	Allows conversations in real time	Does not allow for personal messages
Individual documentation of conversations	Long e-mail threads bury important information	Multiple employees can communicate simultaneously	Individual documentation may be more difficult
	Information not shared as readily	Feedback is instantaneous, eliminating long e-mail chains and increasing productivity	
	More time involved in reading and writing individual e-mail messages	Efficient, single platform for communications	
	Some individuals may be omitted from the e-mail list and do not receive crucial information	Promotes transparency, encourages cross-boundary communications in the organization	
	Information may be transmitted in error or omitted, causing more messages to be sent	Filtering, filing, and retrieval of information is quick and easy	
	Junk mail can take valuable time and space	Encourages engagement of all team members	

FIGURE 3.3

Comparison of advantages and disadvantages of e-mail versus social collaboration.

The availability of social collaboration platforms can provide access to communications for virtual project teams in real time. The benefits include higher employee satisfaction, better knowledge sharing, and increased productivity [30]. Social networking sites and personal social sharing sites that connect individuals one-on-one are not considered social collaboration sites in most business environments. Instead, social collaboration sites involve providing a platform for solving business problems and improving team performance for project teams within an organization. Social collaboration can increase innovation, efficiency, and problem solving when managed by the e-leader for the project, providing a new way to manage, track, and share information for the project and even across projects.

Social networking sites, however, should also be included in this discussion. Facebook, LinkedIn, and MySpace are current examples of social networking that have application to virtual project communications. Using this type of technology, teams can exchange messages and chat, making use of automatic notifications when updates are added. Photos, personal interests, contact information, and other personal information can be added to the social networking page, allowing for more personalized virtual team interaction and development of interpersonal relationships. Social media sites provide for more diverse communication with richer features than e-mail allows. Privacy, confidentiality of intellectual property, and safety of user accounts should be considered when determining if social networking sites are applicable to projects in organizations. Some organizations have found that developing internal wikis, intranets, shared drives, or team web pages have alleviated many of the privacy concerns of social networking and enabled similar activities behind the safety of the organization's firewall. Some monitoring may still be necessary, as cyberbullying, harassment, and other problems may occur, and monitoring of internal sites can often effectively manage these challenges. As a rule, sharing between team members is a healthy and natural way to establish open communication and opportunities for joint problem solving and decision making.

In 1995, Handy [31] wrote this about virtual work: "If there is an office in the future, it will be more like a clubhouse: a place for meetings, eating, and greeting, with rooms reserved for activities, not for particular people." Little did Handy realize that his definition was surprisingly close to the 3-D online virtual world now possible through technologies such as Second Life [32]. Virtual world technologies provide electronic, web-based interaction through avatars (3-D virtual graphic representations). The world (or grid of 3-D geometric shapes and designs) developed for these avatars allows them to interact with each other and participate in group activities and share information in a virtual reality community. Using a virtual world, the organization can create a virtual workplace for teams to interact, meet, communicate, develop ideas and processes, and receive training—all electronically. Technical, legal, pricing, and security issues remain to be resolved with the use of virtual worlds in the business environment, but it is being considered by real-world corporations for banking, training, and e-commerce applications.

Change from traditional communication technologies does not come easily. To successfully install a cloud-based project environment or more advanced technologies, the organization needs to provide change management and training. Teams will need to seek out, learn, and work together to implement new technologies. An organization already using dispersed teams is more likely to adapt to social collaboration than one that is not. Change management processes and training are essential to the success of any technology. The potential, capacity, and capability of social collaboration and social networking to connect individuals make them important tools for organizations.

Not all communication requires high-tech solutions, nor will those solutions be available to all project managers. Simply posting the bio and photo of one team member with each meeting minutes can duplicate some social networking characteristics and is a simple way to build relationships using existing technology. If more elaborate technology is available and the team is trained to use it, employ the technology that supports state-of-the-art communication and collaboration whenever possible.

USING MULTIPLE LEADERSHIP STYLES TO COMMUNICATE TO DISTRIBUTED TEAMS

There is no opportunity to visit at the coffee machine or jog during lunch in the virtual environment. It becomes the project manager's responsibility to build the relationships and communications that are necessary for the virtual team to be successful. Team websites, collaborative tools, and networks that act as virtual water coolers can encourage informal team communication [33]. A mix of communication methods is encouraged in most organizations. Just as there are multiple ways to communicate, there are multiple leadership styles with which to most effectively use communication tools. Being able to match the communication tool to the needs of each individual in the project team is essential to the success of the project.

Situational Communication Styles

An example of a virtual project manager (anonymous) using situational-style communication is shown in the following quote:

> The key is communication. As a project manager you can try to force the team communication into the method that works for you—or you can adjust your communication to what fits each individual. Many people are able to manage their portion of the project with only e-mail and periodic telephone calls—others need you to check in by phone or face-to-face more often.

Another project manager (anonymous) with several years of virtual project management experience states:

> I think that, before all, the PM needs to think out of the box and understand that when he (or she) is working in a virtual project, he (or she) needs to deal with people most of the time away from "official headquarters" (foreign people, people in another city or state) and sometimes we can't use just one communication style because the feeling and impressions of those resources are different.

Still another project manager (anonymous) underscores the necessity of being flexible with communication styles when working with the virtual team:

> A project manager's communication style is a significant factor for successful projects. However, depending on the project type (software, process, organizational change, etc.), team members experience, and project management maturity level of (one or more organizations—e.g., when working with vendors), the most critical component is the ability of the project manager to be a chameleon to adapt their style to get the best out of their project team and partners.

Understanding and analyzing each team member's communication style and needs are important to the success of the project and the trust and relationships built by the project manager. The project manager can use any available personality-type index or style tool, such as Merrill's style characteristics or the Myers-Briggs Type Indicator (MBTI), to identify the characteristics of each team member. Understanding the primary personality styles of each team member, such as analytical-thinker, driver-results, amiable-pleaser, or expressive-needs, will result in better communication for the individual, the e-leader, and the team. Using the results to blend the team and provide the best mode of communication for each individual, the project manager can adjust to the maturity of the team member and become more flexible in the type of communication that is needed, depending upon the individual. For example, the "analytical" may respond well to collaboration databases and issues management bulletin boards. The "driver" on the virtual team often finds it difficult to listen, so asynchronous communications, such as e-mail, messaging, and texting, may be the best communication media. The "amiable" virtual team member may be a good listener, sensitive, and patient. Good communication styles for this member may include video- and tele-conferencing. The "expressive" team member may need more informal contact with the team and e-leader, because of the sociable, personable, and emotional nature of this individual. This team member may respond well to chats, social media, and videoconferencing. Videoconferencing, however, must be prescheduled, which may detract from the expressive-type team member's need for informal, personable communication. The manager may choose to have the virtual project team share their individual MBTI types with each other and suggest that the team members attempt to communicate with the other individuals on the team in the best medium for that individual. Table 3.6 is an easy checklist to provide team members with the communication preference for each Merrill-Reid (1999) personality style.

TABLE 3.6

Virtual Communication Preferences by Merrill-Reid personality style

MBTI Characteristic	Virtual Communication Preference
Analytical-Thinker	Collaboration databases
	Issues management bulletin boards
Driver-Results	e-Mail
	Text
	Messaging
Amiable-Pleaser	Videoconferencing
	Teleconferencing
Expressive-Needs	Chats, social media
	Videoconferencing

Source: Merrill, D.W., & Reid, R. H. (1999). *Personal Styles & Effective Performance.* Boca Raton, FL: CRC Press.

Access to instant messaging and text messaging tools allows the project manager to work more closely with less-experienced team members who may need closer supervision and immediate communication. These team members will appreciate the attention and responsiveness of the project manager, and the relationship built becomes one of trust and respect between the e-leader and the team member. A more mature team member, however, may consider the constancy of instant messages and texts as invasive, considering it micromanaging by the e-leader and leading to an unsuccessful relationship between the e-leader and team member and, possibly, a decrease in productivity by the mature team member or loss of the mature team member.

Servant Leadership Communication

The servant-leader shares power, engages the team in participative decision making, puts the needs of others first, and encourages individual development. It is important that the e-leader take time to listen to each team member. For remote team members, sharing a sympathetic ear to discuss issues, problems, and frustrations may eliminate issues later in the project. It is difficult to pick up on these nuances virtually, and extra effort needs to be made by the project manager to decipher what is and is not important when listening to feedback from the team.

Providing the opportunity for team members to edit or correct the minutes from team meetings is one way to involve the team and encourage feedback. Encouraging participative decision making through the use of multiple avenues of communication using several tools, the e-leader can guide the team toward success. Suggestions for participative communication [34] are listed below:

- Conduct frequent check-ins.
- Ask questions using a Likert scale of 1–5 to draw out all team members.
- Ask open-ended questions.
- Ask team members to repeat.
- Follow up with phone calls and e-mails.

Communication with Empowerment

The virtual team leader can use empowerment leadership techniques to enhance communications and promote emerging leadership within the team. The self-managing team still needs clear direction and goal setting, and the e-leader provides the organization's rules, guidelines, and procedures regarding document management, collaboration databases, cloud, or company databases.

The e-leader using an empowerment leadership style should focus on getting the team to collaboratively clarify expectations regarding shared leadership [35]. Recognizing the multiple skill levels, experience, and specializations within the team, a skills database can be developed and placed online for all the virtual team members to access. A video- or teleconference with the team can define which individuals are willing to share leadership for which tasks or stage of the project. As the virtual project leader, the project manager usually takes the responsibility for leading virtual meetings, managing communications, and monitoring progress toward the deliverables' goals. However, leadership may move to a virtual team member as the work progresses. For the empowered team, a website with information located within easily navigable tabs [36] indicating the following can be used as a guide to developing shared leadership and communications:

- Purpose (team charter, goals, vision, deliverable requirements)
- Team (team member roles, leadership responsibilities, team skills database, interpersonal communications, team member contact information)
- Processes (work breakdown structure, monitoring and controlling processes, quality measurements, risk and issues logs, communication plan for disseminating project information)
- Meetings (schedule of meetings and who has responsibility for leading, taking minutes, coordinating, scheduling)
- Communications (updates, links, reports, minutes)
- Schedule (project schedule, timelines, Gantt charts, vacation and holiday schedules)
- Project work (working documents, deliverables)

Making this information readily available online for the team will provide emerging and assigned leaders with the information they need to be successful. Emergent leaders should surface and can be encouraged through the use of social collaboration and networking, in addition to the team website.

Entrepreneurial Leadership Communication Skills

The entrepreneurial leader needs to communicate the vision for the project, facilitate problem solving, manage strategic initiatives, and encourage decision making and risk taking. This is a leader who is able to organize others to get things done. Collaboration databases, cloud, or company databases can assist in providing the entrepreneurial virtual leader the means by which to communicate necessary information.

If the team is made up of individuals who communicate and act like entrepreneurs, then they are more apt to think strategically and manage tasks alone, and the organization's executives need to provide platforms and infrastructures that support the freelance communication style.

Issues and risk logs are excellent tools for the virtual project manager leading a team of entrepreneurial-type individuals. The issues log is like a problem and solution forum—new issues are identified and current issues are solved and documented in this log [37]. Think of issues as concerns affecting the project or variances that the project manager and team resolve. (What caused the variance? How was it resolved? Hint: Think *past* and *present*.) An example of an issues log is shown in Figure 3.4.

The risk log is an extension of the risk response plan. The risk response plan sets out the action plan to mitigate the risks identified for the team. The risk log helps monitor that these actions happen. It can establish the risk baseline, evaluate the actual risk status, and then define the actual actions taken [38]. Think of the risk log as things that you need to prevent or mitigate. (Hint: Think *future*.) The best practices for monitoring and controlling risk are often the simplest tools, such as the Gantt chart or control chart. An example of a risk log is shown in Figure 3.5.

Automating the monitoring and reporting processes for issues and risk logs can be done with Excel worksheets, Lotus Notes databases, or other tools that are easily accessed by the virtual team. More complex risk monitoring and control techniques, such as variance and trend analyses (Monte Carlo simulations, earned value, etc.), require the use of performance data and may be more appropriate for the project manager and project management office.

The main communication mechanism for managing risks and issues is good discussion and communication on the project team. Processes should be in place to ensure open communication during the monitor and control project process [39]. Project status teleconferences, Twitter updates, e-mails, and published logs on the project's website are simple and effective

Issue #/WBS#	Description	Impact	Date Opened	Originator	Owner	Status (O/C)	Date Closed

FIGURE 3.4
Issues log.

Risk #/WBS#	Description	Risk Impact/ Probability Rank	Date Opened	Owner	Proposed Risk Response	Response Implemented? Y/N	Date Closed

FIGURE 3.5
Risk log.

Ref. #/WBS#	Date	Category (technical, process, etc.)	Decision	Owner	Status (O/C)	Date Closed	Comments

FIGURE 3.6
Decision log.

ways to communicate risks and issues to the project team. If entrepreneurs are on the project team, or a leader with an entrepreneurial management style, the tendency to think strategically, manage tasks alone, and assume risk drives the need for these logs as an important part of the communications plan and processes. To manage this, the project manager can designate a decision log on the shared database of the project (Figure 3.6).

LOOKING AHEAD: CULTURAL COMMUNICATION ISSUES AND EFFECTIVE E-LEADERSHIP

The impact of multiple cultures on communications in the virtual team is significant enough to merit a separate chapter of this book—Chapter 4. As the 21st century unfolds, global growth continues to present challenges. Organizations will begin to see major imbalances in the skills and labor market and will look to global workers and global leadership to maintain a competitive advantage. The workforce of the future needs and wants to be mobile [40]. Years ago John Chambers, CEO of Cisco, summarized the importance of understanding culture in communications for global leaders: "Globally linked virtual teams will transform every government and company in the world. Any of our peers who don't do it won't survive" [41].

Case Study 3.1: Jorge Makes the Switch to a Virtual Communication Plan

OVERVIEW

Jorge is a project manager for a large electronics company. As a project manager for traditional, collocated projects, he relies heavily upon oral communication (face-to-face, team meetings), telephone, e-mail, and hard copies (paper) for reports, memos, and letters. Yesterday Jorge was given his first hybrid virtual project. Several of the team members are virtual and in different time zones. Only Jorge and two team members are collocated at the organization's headquarters. He immediately realizes that his tried-and-true project communication plan template will need to change.

DEBRIEF

Jorge begins to sketch out his thoughts regarding how he will communicate with his dispersed project team. Realizing the importance of a good communications plan, he drafts his ideas for the communication plan in a table format (Table 3.7) to share with the team.

He quickly realizes that his draft looks just like his tried-and-true traditional collocated project communications plans and modifies it by adding one more column to the table (Table 3.8)—to answer the *where* for each piece of his plan.

It is immediately evident that he is going to need the company to set up some kind of collaborative database for his project that all his team members and stakeholders can access. He sets up a meeting to talk with the IT department about what his needs will be for this database. He also decides to talk with them to determine the *how* of communicating with his new team. He presents them the following needs for communication technology [1]:

1. Voicemail and e-mail for updates and information sharing (low-interaction activities)
2. Electronic bulletin board, chat room, website, and video- and audio-conferencing for brainstorming, problem solving, and decision making (moderate-interaction activities)
3. Conferencing with audio/video and text/graphic, whiteboards with audio/video link, collaborative writing tools with audio/video links, and electronic meeting system (EMS) with audio/video and text and graphic support for collaborative work (high-interaction activities)

After the team's kickoff meeting, Jorge knows he will need to involve the team in putting together the final version of their communications plan. As he always does with his teams, he will be asking for their help in developing the communications plan. He will involve them in deciding what messages need to be conveyed and who needs to get them, the frequency of the communications, the level of detail needed, and the outcome of the communications. With this team, however, he decides the most important questions he will be asking are, "What is the best format for each audience and message?" and "What is the best medium for each audience and message?" Understanding that several

TABLE 3.7

Jorge's Communications Plan Draft

Type of Communication	Purpose of Communication	Owner	Audience	Frequency	Documentation
Project Status Meeting	Update work plan, issue resolution, project status	Project Manager	Project Team	Weekly	Meeting Minutes
Issues Log	Issue monitoring	Project Manager and Project Team	Project Team	Ongoing	Issues Log Database
Ongoing Project Status	Show project schedule/status as a whole	Project Manager or Team Lead	Project Team	As needed	Report
Formal Project Status	Show project status as a whole	Project Manager/Team Lead	Stakeholders, Sponsors, Steering Committee	Every 3 weeks or as determined in communications plan	Report
Stakeholders–Sponsors Project Status Meeting	Establish if project is on track and is meeting expectations	Project Manager	Stakeholders, Project Sponsors, Project Team	Every 4 weeks or as determined in communications plan	Report for Stakeholders/Sponsors
Lessons Learned	Evaluate the project	Project Manager or Mediator	Project Team	At the end of each project phase, or at the halfway point of the project and at the end of the project	Lessons Learned Database

TABLE 3.8

Jorge's Modified Columns to the Communications Plan

Type of Communication	Documentation	Where?
Project Status Meeting	Meeting Minutes	Company collaboration database
Issues Log	Issues Log Database	Company collaboration database
Ongoing Project Status	Report	Company collaboration database
Formal Project Status	Report	Company collaboration database
Stakeholders–Sponsors Project Status Meeting	Report for Stakeholders/ Sponsors	Company collaboration database
Lessons Learned	Lessons Learned database	Company collaboration database

virtual members of the team have been on virtual teams before, Jorge is ready to listen to their suggestions and allow emergent leaders to come forward with information and ideas for the plan.

Case Study 3.2: Face-to-Face in Action

[As told to the author by "K," who worked for many years as a virtual human resources representative for a large US-based software organization (anonymous interview)]

OVERVIEW

In my organization, the consultants attended four mandatory days in the office every month to attend project meetings to set scope, budget, work breakdown structure (WBS), requirements, and all. Otherwise we were totally virtual. Once every quarter everyone came to an actual office, where we shared project info, milestones, business, profits, best practices, and all. During these meetings, our consultants arrived and left at different times to accommodate one-on-one meetings with leadership. But we all got together at least once during this time for the quarterly meeting. Sometimes leadership would fly to us, or we would fly there. They were really flexible and sensitive to virtual work—very interactively hands-off—they knew they had no control and sometimes got jealous because they were bound to the office! But they would pull all the consultants in regularly for on-ground meetings. They would bring everybody in and say, "What's been going on? What's been good or bad? What needs to change? What can't change?" I know in the military they call it a *debrief*, and maybe that's the same word you'd use here—that's just what we did.

DEBRIEF

K's organization, involved in IT work, called their employees *consultants*. The consultants were treated like entrepreneurs within the company and given ownership of projects. Each consultant was considered very experienced and had at a minimum seven years of experience in his or her specialization. A project manager was assigned by expertise and need, and all the consultants were trained in the company's project management methodology. Teams were given autonomy, and the virtual workers monitored themselves. The organization illustrates entrepreneurial and empowerment leadership styles and was very successful in managing software development projects virtually.

K says: "The consultants attended four mandatory days in the office every month." Monthly mandatory office days were required to help the consultants stay connected to the organization and provide support for project work. The organization had a strong mentoring program, and often the quarterly meeting time was used for mentoring, human resource updates, training, and relationship building. K's organization would use this time during the planning phase of a virtual project to hold project meetings to set scope, determine budget, develop the initial work breakdown structure, and determine project requirements.

Face-to-face meetings with all the organization's consultants were required quarterly. K says: "Once every quarter everyone came to an actual office, where we shared project info, milestones, business, profits, best practices, and all." During quarterly meetings leadership would gauge the progress of the projects, set the vision for the organization, and build trust and relationships. Leadership was able to enhance virtual communication and productivity using these quarterly meetings with the consultants, and also use the time to identify and resolve problems and set leadership expectations. K suggests that the leadership used this time to listen and learn: "They would bring everybody in and say, 'What's been going on? What's been good or bad? What needs to change? What can't change?'"

In this case study, we also see leadership using the quarterly meeting time as a "revolving door" for one-on-one meetings with the consultants. By staggering the times when the consultants arrived and departed from the quarterly meeting location, the leadership was able to provide personal contact time with each consultant.

FOOD FOR THOUGHT

1. Evaluate the benefits of face-to-face communications for the virtual project team. What options does the project manager have if meeting in person with a team member is not possible?
2. Draft a communications plan for a hypothetical virtual project. How does it differ from a traditional project communications plan?
3. Write an e-mail to your virtual team announcing an upcoming tele-conference. Check your e-mail against the rules for Netiquette and correct subject line, body, and closing.

NOTES

Anonymous quotes from virtual project managers are taken from survey responses in:

Lee, M. R. (2011). *e-Leadership for project managers: A study of situational leadership and virtual project success.* ProQuest, UMI Dissertation Publishing.

Anonymous interviews:

Lee, M. R. (2013). *Interviews by M. R. Lee* [Tape recording.] Springfield, IL.

REFERENCES

1. Pulley, M. L., Sessa, V. I., Fleenor, J., & Pohlmann, T. (2001). e-Leadership: Separating the reality from the hype. *Leadership in Action—LIA,* 21(4), 3–6.
2. Rad, P. F., & Levin, G. (2003). *Achieving project management success using virtual teams.* Boca Raton, FL: J. Ross Publishing, Inc.
3. Gibson, C., & Cohen, S. (2003). *Virtual teams that work: Creating conditions for virtual team effectiveness.* San Francisco: Jossey-Bass.
4. Project Management Institute. (2007). *Project manager competency development framework* (2nd ed.). Newton Square, PA: Project Management Institute.
5. Project Management Institute. (2013). *A guide to the project management body of knowledge: PMBOK guide* (5th ed.). Newton Square, PA: Project Management Institute.

6. McLeod, K. (2004, February 25). Communication in the workplace. AllPM.com. Retrieved from http://www.allpm.com.
7. Sarker, S., & Sahay, S. (2003). Understanding virtual team development: An interpretive study. *Journal of the Association for Information Systems*, 4(1), 1–36.
8. Goodbody, J. (2005). Critical success factors for global virtual teams. *Strategic Communication Management*, 9(2), 18–21.
9. Project Management Institute. (2013). *A guide to the project management body of knowledge: PMBOK guide* (5th ed.). Newton Square, PA: Project Management Institute.
10. Dick, W., & Carey, L. (1996). *The systematic design of instruction* (4th ed.). New York: Harper Collins.
11. Haywood, M. (2000). Working in virtual teams: A tale of two projects and many cities. *IT Professional Magazine*, 2(2), 58–60.
12. Griffin, S. D. (2002). A taxonomy of Internet applications for project management communication. *Project Management Journal*, 33(4), 39–47.
13. Garton, C., & Wegryn, K. (2006). *Managing without walls*. Lewisville, TX: Mc Press Online, LP.
14. Zakaria, N., Amelinckx, A., & Wilemon, D. (2004). Working together apart? Building a knowledge-sharing culture for global virtual teams. *Creativity and Innovation Management*, 13(1), 15–29.
15. Duarte, D., & Snyder, N. (1999). *Mastering virtual teams*. San Francisco: Jossey-Bass.
16. Verma, V. K. (1996). *Human Resource Skills for the Project Manager*. Newton Square, PA: Project Management Institute.
17. Rad, P. F., & Levin, G. (2003). *Achieving project management success using virtual teams*. Boca Raton, FL: J. Ross Publishing, Inc.
18. Garton, C., & Wegryn, K. (2006). *Managing without walls*. Lewisville, TX: Mc Press Online, LP.
19. Garton, C., & Wegryn, K. (2006). *Managing without walls*. Lewisville, TX: Mc Press Online, LP.
20. Mayer, M. (2010). *The virtual edge: Embracing technology for distributed project team success*. Newtown Square, PA: Project Management Institute.
21. Goodbody, J. (2005). Critical success factors for global virtual teams. *Strategic Communication Management*, 9(2), 18–21.
22. Haywood, M. (2000). Working in virtual teams: A tale of two projects and many cities. *IT Professional Magazine*, 2(2), 58–60.
23. Knowledge@Wharton. (2009, September 2). Locals, cosmopolitans and other keys to creating successful global teams. *Knowledge@Wharton*. Retrieved from http://knowledge.wharton.upenn.edu/article.cfm?articleid = 2328.
24. Zofi, Y. S. (2011). *A manager's guide to virtual teams*. New York: AMACOM.
25. Mayer, M. (2010). *The virtual edge: Embracing technology for distributed project team success*. Newtown Square, PA: Project Management Institute.
26. Driskell, J. E., Radtke, P. H., & Salas, E. (2003). Virtual teams: Effects of technological mediation on team performance. *Group Dynamics: Theory, Research, and Practice*, 7(4), 297–323.
27. Driskell, J. E., Radtke, P. H., & Salas, E. (2003). Virtual teams: Effects of technological mediation on team performance. *Group Dynamics: Theory, Research, and Practice*, 7(4), 297–323.

28. Boutellier, R., Gassmann, O., Macho, H., & Roux, M. (1998). Management of dispersed product development teams: The role of information technologies. *R & D Management, 28*(1), 13–25.

29. Khan, D. (2012, December 12). To e-mail or to collaborate: Unlocking value of social collaboration. *CMS Wire*. Retrieved from http://www.cmswire.com/cms/social-business/to-email-or-to-collaborate-unlocking-value-of-social-collaboration-018766.php?goback =%2Egde_2320211_member_196325925.

30. Khan, D. (2012, December 12). To e-mail or to collaborate: Unlocking value of social collaboration. *CMS Wire*. Retrieved from http://www.cmswire.com/cms/social-business/to-email-or-to-collaborate-unlocking-value-of-social-collaboration-018766.php?goback =%2Egde_2320211_member_196325925.

31. Handy, C. (1995). Trust and the virtual organization. *Harvard Business Review, 73*, 40.

32. Linden Research. (2013). What is Second Life? Second Life. Retrieved from http://secondlife.com/whatis/.

33. DeRosa, D. M., & Lepsinger, R. (2010). *Virtual team success: A practical guide for working and leading from a distance.* San Francisco: Jossey-Bass.

34. Zofi, Y. S. (2011). *A manager's guide to virtual teams.* New York: AMACOM.

35. Lipnack, J., & Stamps, J. (2010). *Leading virtual teams: Expert solutions to everyday challenges.* Boston: Harvard Business Press.

36. Lipnack, J., & Stamps, J. (2010). *Leading virtual teams: Expert solutions to everyday challenges.* Boston: Harvard Business Press.

37. Project Management Institute. (2013). *A guide to the project management body of knowledge: PMBOK guide* (5th ed.). Newton Square, PA: Project Management Institute.

38. Milosevic, D. Z. (2003). *Project management toolbox: Tools and techniques for the practicing project manager.* Hoboken, NJ: Wiley & Sons, Inc.

39. Chapman, C., & Ward, S. (2003). *Project risk management: Processes, techniques and insights.* Hoboken, NJ: John Wiley and Sons.

40. Bersin, J. (2013). HR, leadership, technology, and talent management predictions for 2013. *Forbes.* Retrieved from www.forbes.com/sites/joshbersin/2013/01/11/hr-leadership.

41. Wiener, N. (1950). *The human use of human beings.* New York: Anchor Books.

CASE STUDY REFERENCE

1. Duarte, D., & Snyder, N. (1999). *Mastering virtual teams.* San Francisco: Jossey-Bass.

4

Cultural Communication Issues and Effective e-Leadership

"Global teams are like oceans: Depending on how they are navigated, they can link the world together or split it apart" [1]. Navigating those "oceans" for the virtual project manager is crucial to the success of the project. Global teams with team members from various cultures bring new challenges for the e-leaders of projects. Globalization also provides the opportunity to manage a more diverse, higher-quality talent pool. The multicultural organization is "argued to be more effective at innovation and problem-solving" [2]. The virtual project manager can capitalize on this diversity to improve performance on project teams by recognizing, encouraging, and employing the varied talents of the diverse multicultural project team. The e-leader of multicultural project teams must have a foundational understanding of the basic dimensions of culture, how culture affects the organization, and the importance of integrating the organizational culture with global cultures. With that knowledge, the virtual project manager needs to develop the competencies, tools, and techniques to successfully charter the waters of communication across cultures. The flexibility of management styles and the ability to match the communications and e-leadership to the situation, culture, and individual will bring the project safely to shore.

UNDERSTANDING CULTURE

Leading global project management teams requires understanding cultural differences, shared common goals, and communication preferences.

Culture is defined as "the collective programming of the mind which distinguishes the members of one group from another" [3]. Culture can be revealed differently depending upon religious beliefs, nationality, ethnicity, gender, age, organizational identity, bias, assumptions, worldviews, and communication patterns. In our modern world, most individuals will communicate with people from different cultures at some point, and the quality of these interactions affects how the communications are interpreted and acted upon. Each interaction provides the opportunity to learn and grow in developing the competencies to become a global communicator. Personal cultural traditions and beliefs influence all interpersonal interactions, and developing a deeper understanding of culture is necessary in our global environment today.

The term *culture* can include many different concepts. Culture can loosely refer to groups ranging from Asian American culture to deaf culture to the culture of the rich to southern culture. Identifying culture as "the totality of learned, shared symbols, language, values, and norms that distinguish one group of people from another" [4] is a usable and general description of how culture affects individuals as they interact with each other. By identifying cultures in this manner, the emphasis is on the individuals in the culture, not on specific nationalities and ethnicities. Culture is not something that is inherited genetically, such as hair color or physical characteristics. Culture or enculturation is learned and acquired through symbols, language, beliefs, customs, values, and norms developed over a lifetime.

Belonging to a culture does not prevent an individual from belonging to *co-cultures*. Co-cultures, sometimes also called subcultures, exist within larger cultures and are exemplified by smaller groups that share activities, beliefs, interests, traditions, and mental or physical abilities. The co-cultures a person belongs to shape the individuality of the person within the larger culture. An individual can identify with more than one co-culture, and co-cultures can be quite varied, from the business organization the person works for to the clubs that person belongs to. Companies can be organizational cultures, and teams can become co-cultures within the company. Often people in co-cultures will identify themselves to distinguish their identity from others by wearing a symbol, such as the pink triangle used by gay, lesbian, bisexual, and transgender (GLBT) individuals, or with certain jargon used only by their group [5].

Primary Dimensions of Culture

Much research has been done on the topic of culture, and six dimensions of culture have been identified that influence how people communicate and interact with each other [6]. These primary dimensions are essential to understanding global project management and e-leadership. The six cultural dimensions are as follows:

- Individualistic versus Collectivistic Cultures
- Low-Context versus High-Context Cultures
- Low-Power Distance versus High-Power Distance Cultures
- Masculine versus Feminine Cultures
- Monochronic versus Polychronic Cultures
- Low Uncertainty Avoidance versus High Uncertainty Avoidance Cultures

Each dimension relates to a particular type of communication, interaction, or way in which the culture reacts to a specific situation, as illustrated in Figure 4.1.

Individualistic versus Collectivistic Cultures

Figure 4.2 illustrates the Relationship Orientation dimension—individualistic and collectivistic cultures. In an *individualistic* culture, individuals believe that their primary responsibility is to themselves, and they value self-reliance and self-sufficiency. The emphasis is on *self*. This does not mean that the person is selfish or self-centered, but that the focus of growth and development is on the individual and not a team or group of people. The United States, Canada, Great Britain, and Australia are examples of individualistic cultures [7]. A team member from an individualistic culture may look for help from the project manager with career development or presenting work results to functional managers. Individuals in *collectivistic cultures*, such as Korea, Japan, and many countries in Africa and Latin America, reflect the belief that their primary responsibility is to family, community, and employers. The emphasis is on caring for the needs of the group before the needs of oneself. If the team, family, or group in the collectivistic culture is to do well, then everyone must be involved in making the team, family, or group successful. Individuals from collectivistic cultures take credit for work done by the team, not for individual contributions to the team.

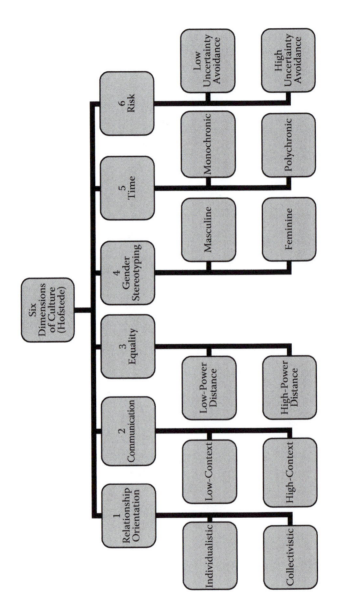

FIGURE 4.1

Six dimensions of culture (Hofstede).

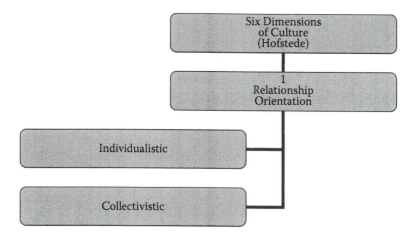

FIGURE 4.2

Six dimensions of culture (Hofstede): Relationship orientation—individualistic and collectivistic.

In communicating, individuals in individualistic cultures openly express conflict and work toward resolution. They often stand up for themselves and state their individual preferences without hesitation. They are more likely to work independently and prefer less interaction and participation with others on the team or in the group. These individuals respond well to most forms of communication but often prefer e-mail, reports, and status updates to meetings. Individuals in collectivistic cultures may be more apt to be indirect in communicating and attempt to resolve conflict by compromise and blending into the group. These individuals tend to prefer face-to-face communications, videoconferencing, teleconferencing, and group meetings. The virtual project manager has the responsibility to clearly define the degree of interaction and participation that is appropriate for the team when working with individuals from collectivistic cultures and individualistic cultures, including the type of interactive behavior, frequency of interactions, and amount of participation expected [8]. Prompts and "rules" about participation in communications will help individuals from collectivistic cultures recognize that it is acceptable to speak out regarding individual conflicts, preferences, and personal needs during project work.

Low-Context versus High-Context Cultures

Figure 4.3 illustrates the Communication dimension—low-context and high-context cultures. In the *low-context culture*, individuals are expected

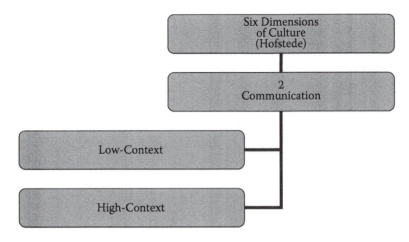

FIGURE 4.3
Six dimensions of culture (Hofstede): Communication—low-context and high-context.

to say what they mean and communicate directly. The low-context cultures are predominately task oriented. In the low-context culture, a leader may be direct and explicit about a team member's performance problems and expectations for improvement, giving examples of the individual's work performance. The United States, Israel, Canada, and most northern European countries are considered low-context cultures. In organizations, functional areas with subcultures of low context may include engineering, finance, or administrative services. Low-context cultures generally communicate well in any type of synchronous or asynchronous situation but prefer asynchronous communications [9].

In the *high-context culture*, individuals are expected to speak in an indirect, ambiguous, and inexplicit manner, causing a reluctance to speak negatively or say no. The high-context cultures are predominately relationship oriented. The emphasis in the high-context culture is maintaining harmony and not being offensive. In a high-context culture, the leader may opt for a private "talk" that focuses on a team member's performance problems and addresses how the issues affect the other team members and the productivity of the entire group. High-context cultures can be found in Korea, the Maori of New Zealand, and Native Americans [10]. Some functional areas within an organization may be high-context subcultures. Examples of functional groups in organizations tending to be high-context would be human resources, marketing, or training and development. High-context cultures generally communicate best through media-rich, synchronous communication channels, including face-to-face, teleconferences, and videoconferences. Individuals from high-context cultures may enjoy social networking, blogs, and chat rooms as a means of communicating with other team members.

The team member from the high-context culture may be just invoking her or his preference in communications by not being direct in answering questions or constantly agreeing with everything that is said by the team. However, this can be perceived as an insult and a lack of confidence in other team members' competence by low-context culture individuals who are looking for a direct and straightforward response, and can therefore erode trust on the team. The multicultural project manager should be aware of these differences and, using the communications plan as a tool, develop a process to eliminate this challenge by clearly defining the expectations for open communication on the global team.

Low-Power Distance versus High-Power Distance Cultures

Figure 4.4 illustrates the Equality dimension—low-power distance and high-power distance cultures. Power in society, organizations, or teams varies widely in low-power distance and high-power distance cultures. Equality in education, equality for co-cultures, and equality for sexes are ideals widely embraced by most democratic societies, such as the United States, Canada, New Zealand, Denmark, Austria, and most western European countries. These cultures believe that all individuals are equal

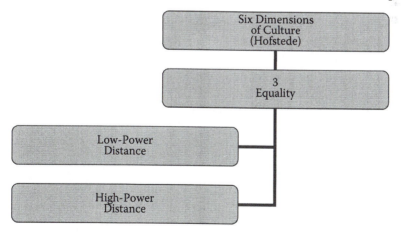

FIGURE 4.4

Six dimensions of culture (Hofstede): Equality—low-power distance and high-power distance.

and that no one person or group controls through excessive power, and are considered *low-power distance* cultures. *High-power distance* cultures show a preference for distributing power to certain individuals based upon their position in society or politics. Power is not distributed equally but is given to certain individuals, and respect for the individuals with power is expected from everyone or else there are consequences. China, Thailand, Mexico, Brazil, India, Singapore, and the Philippines are examples of high-power distance cultures [11].

Many aspects of life are differentiated by the low- and high-power distance cultures. Friendships and romantic relationships are usually based on love in low-power distance societies but may be based on social status and social class in high-power distance cultures. Individuals in high-power distance cultures tend to obey and respect authority. Individuals in low-power distance cultures are more apt to question authority and do what they think is right. In organizations, low-power distance culture employees prefer to work autonomously but be involved in decisions, providing input and suggestions for the organization. Individuals from high-power distance cultures expect their employers to make all decisions and to tell them how to do their job and do not expect to provide input or ideas for the organization. Team members from high-power distance cultures often accept decisions from others on the team who appear to have more power, without first consulting the team or the project manager. This can cause tension and trust issues in the team, especially in low-power distance cultures. The project manager needs to provide clear guidelines as to decision-making and problem-solving procedures for the multicultural team.

The fact that the multicultural team is virtual is an advantage for teams with cultural differences in power distance. Virtual project managers can use technology to minimize these differences in the team. Team members from high-power distance cultures engage more readily in asynchronous technologies [12]. Individuals from high-power distance cultures may be more apt to share their ideas via e-mail or surveys, where power can be perceived as anonymous or not an issue. Instant audience feedback technologies that allow "voting" through a smart device or laptop provide another option for individuals with high-power distance culture issues. Virtual technology places the focus on the ideas, opinions, and perspectives and decreases the focus on culture, position, and titles [13]. Collaborative software enables contributions and comments without regard for position or authority. Virtual work provides a small window of anonymity that can help the high-power distance team members save face to become better contributors.

Masculine versus Feminine Cultures

Figure 4.5 illustrates the Gender-Stereotyping dimension—masculine and feminine cultures. Traditional masculine values and sex-specific roles define the *masculine culture.* Austrian, Japanese, and Mexican cultures expect high-wage and decision-making positions in organizations to be held by men and positions of nurturer (nurse, homemaker, mother) to be held by women. Individuals from masculine cultures may prefer to communicate using asynchronous technology. They also tend to be more competitive and may use phrases such as "kill the competition" or "we'll destroy them" when discussing project work.

Feminine cultures do not differentiate male and female roles. They encourage equality of sexes and discourage sexual stereotypes. Individuals from feminine cultures may prefer communicating with technology that provides opportunities to coach and nurture, such as telephone calls, videoconferencing or face-to-face meetings, especially during the start-up phase of projects. Chile, Sweden, and the Netherlands are examples of feminine cultures [14]. The same anonymity that provides a means by which to lessen the challenges of working with high-power distance cultures can also prove valuable in mitigating differences between masculine and feminine cultures on the virtual project team. Surveys, polls, e-mails, collaborative databases, and collaborative documents are tools the project manager can use to build trust and relationships between individuals from masculine and feminine cultures.

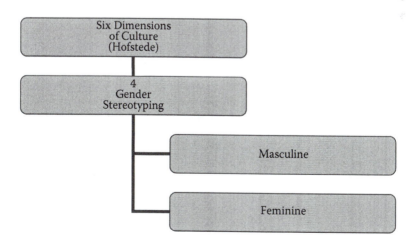

FIGURE 4.5

Six dimensions of culture (Hofstede): Gender stereotyping—masculine and feminine.

Monochronic versus Polychronic Cultures

Time, so important to the schedules and deadlines in the project life cycle, is also considered a dimension that defines many cultures (see Figure 4.6). The *monochronic culture* (Swiss, German, and U.S.) views time as a finite and tangible commodity. The *polychronic culture* (Latin American, Arab Middle Eastern, and some sub-Saharan African) views time as flowing, holistic, fluid, and never ending. For a meeting, the individuals from the monochronic culture may arrive at a specific time or five minutes early. For the same meeting, the individuals from the polychronic culture may arrive over a period of time or within a time frame of morning or afternoon. This diversity should be addressed by the organization and by the project manager, with expectations and time management explicitly explained for members from polychronic cultures. Communications in a monochronic culture can be asynchronous or synchronous. Communications in a poly-chronic culture can be asynchronous; but if synchronous, the project manager needs to set specific expectations for engagement. Misunderstandings about cultural time can cause challenges for the multicultural global team. Team members from polychronic cultures might be considered lazy, uninterested, or inefficient by team members from the monochronic cultures. The opposite may also be found—that team members from the mono-chronic cultures may be considered assertive, aggressive, and overambitious by the team members from the polychronic cultures.

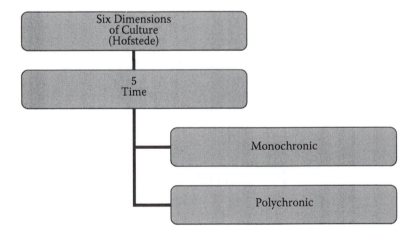

FIGURE 4.6
Six dimensions of culture (Hofstede): Time—monochronic and polychronic.

Low Uncertainty Avoidance versus High Uncertainty Avoidance Cultures

Figure 4.7 illustrates the Risk dimension—low uncertainty avoidance and high uncertainty avoidance cultures. Most people try to avoid uncomfortable situations, and the extent by which they try to avoid anything unfamiliar, unstructured, unclear, or unpredictable is termed *uncertainty avoidance*. Individuals from cultures and co-cultures where new situations, opportunities, choices, and ideas are accepted easily are considered *low uncertainty avoidance*. Hong Kong, Jamaica, and New Zealand are examples of countries with low uncertainty avoidance cultures. Individuals with *high uncertainty avoidance* tend to stay in situations that are familiar, take few risks, fear failure, and favor rules and laws and security measures that reduce uncertainty in society. Countries that are often considered to have cultures with high uncertainty avoidance are Argentina, Portugal, and Uruguay. The project manager can provide individuals from high uncertainty avoidance cultures with defined plans, schedules, and responsibilities. In addition, the project manager should be sure that the project has collaborative databases where documentation of decisions and records can be accessed.

The virtual e-leader should also provide as much time as necessary for the team to discuss process and documentation, allowing time for those from high uncertainty avoidance cultures to become comfortable with the level of uncertainty. The anxious and uncertain actions of the team

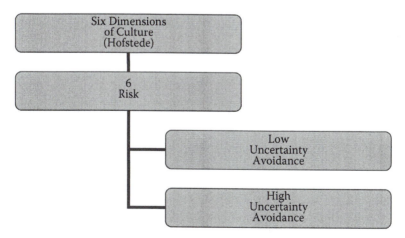

FIGURE 4.7

Six dimensions of culture (Hofstede): Risk—low uncertainty avoidance and high uncertainty avoidance.

members from the high uncertainty avoidance cultures can be interpreted by other members of the team as being distrustful or as not having confidence in the competencies of the other team members. Hesitation in one culture may indicate the person is thinking and analyzing what was said. In another culture it may be a signal of discomfort in what was just said. These unspoken assumptions are fueled by the inability of team members to be able to read and react to nonverbal cues if the conversation is voice-only [15]. By slowing down the discussions about processes and documentation, the virtual project manager can assure the entire team that being prudent in moving forward is a team decision and team activity.

Table 4.1 lists each dimension of culture and primary traits associated with it. Understanding the dimensions of culture is invaluable to the global e-leader.

Table 4.2 lists the dimensions of culture and the example countries for each dimension [16]. Each dimension will become an important input to the communications necessary for global multicultural project team management.

The successful multicultural e-leader should take into consideration the cultural dimension of each team member when reviewing the type of communication that would be most appropriate. In addition, the e-leader should be consistent in the focus when leading those individuals. Table 4.3 displays the cultural dimension, preferred communications for that dimension, and the focus the e-leader should maintain [17] while leading these individuals in the multicultural team.

TABLE 4.1

Cultural Dimensions and Primary Traits Associated with Each

Cultural Dimension	Primary Traits
Individualistic	Self-reliant, self-sufficient
Collectivistic	Group orientation—family, community, company
Low-Context	Direct, task oriented
High-Context	Ambiguous, relationship oriented
Low-Power Distance	Equality, no one person or group holds power
High-Power Distance	Distributed power based on position or politics
Masculine	Traditional male sex-specific roles and responsibilities
Feminine	Traditional female sex-specific roles and responsibilities
Monochronic	Time as finite and tangible
Polychronic	Time as fluid, holistic, and never ending
Low Uncertainty Avoidance	Flexible, adapt to new ideas, take risks
High Uncertainty Avoidance	Avoid uncomfortable situations. Prefer familiar, structured, clear and predictable

TABLE 4.2

Dimensions of Culture and Examples of Countries

Dimension of Culture	Examples of Countries
Individualistic Cultures	United States, Canada, Great Britain, Australia, Netherlands, New Zealand, Italy, Belgium, Denmark
Collectivistic Cultures	Korea, Japan, Guatemala, Ecuador, Panama, Venezuela, Colombia, Indonesia, Pakistan, Costa Rica, Peru, Taiwan
Low-Context Cultures	United States, Israel, Canada, most northern European countries
High-Context Cultures	Korea, India, the Maori of New Zealand, Native Americans, Nigeria, West Africa, Japan
Low-Power Distance Cultures	United States, Canada, New Zealand, Denmark, Austria, Israel, Ireland, Sweden, Norway, Finland, Switzerland
High-Power Distance Cultures	Mexico, Brazil, India, Singapore, Philippines, Malaysia, Guatemala, Panama, Venezuela, Arab countries, Ecuador, Indonesia, China, Thailand
Masculine Cultures	Austria, Japan, Mexico, Venezuela, Italy, Switzerland, Ireland, Jamaica, Great Britain, Germany
Feminine Cultures	Chile, Sweden, Netherlands, Denmark, Costa Rica, Yugoslavia, Finland, Portugal
Monochronic Cultures	Switzerland, Germany, White American, Austria
Polychronic Cultures	Latin America, the Arab part of the Middle East, some areas of sub-Saharan Africa, African American
Low Uncertainty Avoidance Cultures	Hong Kong, Jamaica, New Zealand, Singapore, Denmark, Sweden, Hong Kong, Ireland, Great Britain, Malaysia, India, Philippines, United States
High Uncertainty Avoidance Cultures	Argentina, Portugal, Uruguay, Greece, Guatemala, Belgium, El Salvador, Japan, Yugoslavia, Peru

TABLE 4.3

Cultural Dimensions, Communication Preferences, and Leadership Focus

Cultural Dimension	Predominate Communications Preferences	Leadership Focus
Individualistic	Asynchronous	Allow individuals to talk about themselves first, then discuss how the team members will work together. Allow for autonomy in completing work. Provide collaborative databases, websites, and electronic logs.

(continued)

TABLE 4.3

Cultural Dimensions, Communication Preferences, and Leadership Focus (continued)

Cultural Dimension	Predominate Communications Preferences	Leadership Focus
Collectivistic	Synchronous	Encourage individuals to talk about the team first, then set clear expectations how each individual contributes. Avoid calling attention to the individual apart from the team.
Low-Context	Asynchronous or Synchronous	Allow individuals to discuss their backgrounds and preferences in detail. Provide regular reports and updates electronically.
High-Context	Synchronous	Discuss individuals' backgrounds and preferences in general terms. Provide individual opportunities for one-on-one conversations.
Low-Power Distance	Asynchronous or Synchronous	Use competitive team-building activities. Provide opportunities for autonomous work, yet be involved in decision making and planning and provide input.
High-Power Distance	Synchronous	Use team-building activities that do not disrupt power differences in the team. Provide opportunities to express individual opinions anonymously through individual e-mails, surveys, and instant audience feedback/polls.
Masculine	Asynchronous	Involve individuals in decision making and problem-solving. Allow opportunities for collaboration sites and bulletin boards.
Feminine	Synchronous	Provide opportunities for social networking. Encourage face-to-face, video-, and teleconference meetings. Encourage sharing of ideas, coaching, and mentoring. Take turns starting meetings with someone from the virtual team sharing a story from their country or their part of the project.
Monochronic	Asynchronous	Ensure timely reporting. Provide detailed work schedules.
Polychronic	Synchronous	Encourage meetings, instant messaging, texting, and screen sharing. Provide concrete expectations regarding deadlines, meeting protocol, and documentation.
Low Uncertainty Avoidance	Synchronous	Discuss very generally how the team will work together, then discuss specifics later.
High Uncertainty Avoidance	Asynchronous	Discuss very concretely how the team members will work together. Provide defined plans, schedules, and lists for responsibilities on accessible databases.

CULTURES WITHIN THE ORGANIZATION

Organizational Culture

Organizational culture is defined as "a system of shared meaning held by members" [18] of an organization and is important in characterizing the identity of the organization. Separate from cultural differences stemming from, for example, nationality or geographic location, organizational cultures vary by the assumptions and core beliefs of the actual organization where the team members are employed. The values shared by the individuals in the group and the behavior patterns shape the culture of the organization. Organizational culture provides the norms, standards, values, and behaviors for those within the organization. By defining the identity of the organization, organizational culture also establishes membership of those in the organization and a commitment to the group as a whole. Individuals who do not follow these norms are penalized or removed from the culture. Individuals who follow the cultural norms are rewarded. Motivation is then enhanced and employees become more committed to the organization [19].

The organization's success, therefore, can be directly related to the culture of the organization. Strong, positive cultures have a significant impact on a company's long-term economic performance [20]. The opposite may also be true. A weak, ineffective culture can cause the demise of an organization. An organization's strategic goals typically relate directly to the organization's mission, vision, and values, and these goals bring about additional group cohesiveness, behaviors, and bonding [21]. In turn, the goals strengthen the organizational culture. If the organization's goals are in conflict with the culture, then the opposite may occur and the culture may work against goal attainment [22].

Innovations and changes may influence the culture of an organization, as may new ventures based on innovation or changes resulting from competition or technical advances. Environmental changes, such as globalization, regulations, or workforce diversity, may cause a culture to change or need to be changed. In addition, the age of an organization can represent an internal change that can influence the culture. Older organizations tend to be more standardized and formalized [23]. Limited or aging technology within the organization may reflect an aging culture in an organization. Mechanized and bureaucratic structures may impair the adaptability of the organization. A workforce not trained in 21st century technologies and holding on to business procedures from the 20th century may hold back an organization. A change in culture may be required to consciously make the aging organization more flexible and adaptable to remain competitive in the virtual, global business environment. Updating values and value creation, as a new focus in organizations, may indicate changes in attitude toward human resources and diversity in personnel that are necessary to increase productivity [24]. This focus may also influence changes in culture.

Organizational culture can and does affect the productivity of the project team. The same organization may have distinct cultural differences within the organization that cause some teams to produce and be more successful than other teams, regardless of ethnicity, language, nationality, religion, or other multicultural differences. Bassi and McMurrer [25] developed a model that measures human capital management, instead of traditional measures, to predict the organization's performance. By measuring leadership practices, employee engagement, knowledge accessibility, workforce optimization, and organizational learning capacity, they posit that productivity can be predicted and managed. The metrics of their survey are basic best practices in organizations that develop strong, productive, and successful cultures. These indicators of organizational culture can provide a road map for successful organizations in the current, global environment.

Team Culture

Similar factors for the success of project teams point directly to the development of a successful *team culture*: common purpose, values, and goals; team vision and unified goals; norms; diversity and inclusion; and respect, trust, and appreciation. As one seasoned project manager (anonymous) says, "Effective virtual project management requires strong understanding of the culture of the team—and using that understanding to manage different project situations." Team cultures, which display the distinctive features of co-cultures, are part of every organization. Team cultures can adopt language, values, symbols, and other cultural values and norms, just like organizations. To develop a team culture, the virtual e-leader can use metaphors, ask the team to design a team logo, help develop a strategic plan, or write team mission and vision statements. By developing the work breakdown structure and communications, risk, and quality plans with the team, the virtual project manager will help build the relationships that develop the team's culture. Involving the project team in developing the processes and procedures that will be used for the project allows the team members to be actively involved in the foundational footings of the team culture. These activities will increase the opportunities for relationship building, communication, trust, and cultural integration within the project team.

Early in the project it is recommended that the project manager facilitate a culture discussion with the virtual team. By engaging the team in defining roles and responsibilities, establishing work processes, and discussing operating agreements such as working conditions, hours, authority, delegation, communication patterns, and other culturally determined activities, the project manager can ensure that everyone on the team will have a clear understanding and positive attitude, behaviors, and values that will make the project a success [26]. Asking questions such as what resources each team member needs, how early or late each team member can be contacted, or what holidays are observed can unify the team and build trust and respect between the team members, especially for the team that has individuals from multiple cultures.

A positive team culture makes a huge difference in the success of a project. A positive organizational culture and positive project team culture will support the organization's core values and influence the behavior of its members because the "high degree of sharedness and intensity creates an internal climate of high behavioral control" [27]. This results in cohesiveness, loyalty, and commitment, which translate to higher productivity in the organization.

Boundary Crossing

Within organizations with functional areas that share employees on various project teams (virtual or collocated), the concept of allowing "boundary crossing" [28] in virtual teams becomes essential to the success of projects. Progressive organizations allow and encourage boundary-crossing communication, both with members of functional areas within the organization and often with external organizations, providing a more global view of the business environment. Different functional areas have different individual team cultures within the organization. The individual team cultures make the project team multicultural. The project manager needs to understand and deal with these different cultures within the organization as if the project team is global and the cultures are from different countries or as if the project team members are from different organizations. For example, the company's engineering area may prefer a structured team environment (low context), but the human resources department may prefer a more interactive structure that includes face-to-face meetings or videoconferencing (high context). Understanding the different types of cultures within the functional areas of the organization is essential to the success of the team. Table 4.4 describes general functional areas in an average U.S. company, the primary dimension of culture associated with each, and the preferred communications for the functional area [29].

The virtual team leader has a responsibility to integrate the individual cultures from various functional teams within the organization into a unified project team culture. As one respondent (anonymous) in a recent survey wrote: "You need to feel comfortable crossing silos, even though people might not want you there. It is a fine line of influencing without stepping on too many toes" [30]. For internal boundary crossing to be successful, the organization policies (human resource and internal systems) must support it. Functional, departmental domains or "silos" of power (different departments that do not interact with each other) make integration extremely challenging. Often, individual jobs become highly formalized and standardized to protect these domains, which makes boundary crossing difficult or impossible. Deliberate boundary-sharing and boundary-spanning activities should be part of the organization's culture to promote sharing within the organization and discourage silos of functional areas. Activities that are focused on networking and establishing relationships across functional boundary lines are particularly productive in developing successful boundary-crossing teams, as is any training that increases the e-leaders' and virtual team members' flexibility and cross-cultural communication skills [31]. The ability within the culture for the project manager to cross boundaries and for the project team to share resources is essential to the success of projects in the 21st century business environment. Much of this success depends upon yet another culture within the organization, the project management culture.

Project Management Cultures

There are several types of *project management cultures*: cooperative, isolated, competitive, noncooperative, and fragmented [32]. Understanding a negative or positive project management cultural environment is important to managing successful projects. Some organizations exhibit

TABLE 4.4

Primary Cultural Dimensions and Preferred Communications by Functional Area

Functional Area	Work Effort	Primary Cultural Dimensions	Preferred Communications
Marketing	Creative, deadline driven	High Context, Low Uncertainty Avoidance	Synchronous: Face-to-face, video- or teleconferencing, instant messaging, chat rooms
Engineering	Rational, logical	Individualistic, Low Context, Masculine, Monochronic	Asynchronous: e-Mail, fax, reports, status updates, collaboration sites, bulletin boards
Software Development	Logical, waterfall, or agile development	Individualistic, Low Context, Low Uncertainty Avoidance	Synchronous: e-Mail, instant messaging Asynchronous: e-Mail, reports, schedule updates, collaboration sites, texting
Accounting	Organized, structured	Low Context, Monochronic, High Uncertainty Avoidance	Asynchronous: e-Mail, reports, status updates, collaboration sites
Research and Development	Flexible, long-term focus	High Context, Polychronic, Low Uncertainty Avoidance	Synchronous: Face-to-face, teleconferencing, instant messaging, meetings, screen sharing Asynchronous: Collaboration sites, websites, bulletin boards
Manufacturing	Project focused, sense of urgency	Low Context, High Uncertainty Avoidance	Asynchronous: e-Mail, reports, production updates Synchronous: Face-to-face, teleconferencing, instant messaging, meetings
Training and Development	Creative, flexible	High Context, Feminine, High Uncertainty Avoidance	Synchronous: Face-to-face, video- and teleconferencing, instant messaging, meetings Asynchronous: e-Mail, websites, collaboration sites
Administrative Services	Project focused, autonomous	Low Context, Masculine, High Uncertainty Avoidance	Asynchronous: e-Mail, fax, voicemail
Human Resources	Organizational focus, external focus	High Context, Collectivistic, Feminine	Synchronous: Face-to-face, video- and teleconference meetings

isolated project management cultures where functional units develop their own project management methodologies, with some of these isolated cultures also displaying competitive culture attributes. Examples are projects that are competing for resources, not working together, or not sharing ideas within the organization. Isolated cultures can cause misalignment of projects and result in failure during the execution, monitoring, and controlling processes. Competitive attributes of an organization can positively drive interrelationships between project management and the business strategy [33]. However, internal environmental competitiveness can cause underuse, misuse, or overuse of resources and inefficiencies. In some organizations, it is almost as if the different functional areas are project-based firms (PBFs)—individual companies whose entire entity is project specific, organized around relatively discrete projects [34]. Project managers in noncooperative, fragmented cultures such as these face the difficult challenges of limited resources, duplication of effort, and lack of cross-functional flexibility. It is important for project managers to understand the internal project management cultural environment and attempt to work around it, without it, or with it to ensure successful projects, especially if the projects are managed virtually.

For the project manager in the organization with isolated, competitive, noncooperative, or fragmented project management cultures, the establishment of a project management office (PMO) is a possible solution. The PMO can define and develop project management standards, provide databases for project documentation, provide training and guidance for project managers, and establish a unified methodology for projects in the organization. This coordination can eliminate the isolated project management cultures, and require governance that provides consistency and continuity between projects. Some PMOs will manage shared resources, eliminating the competition for resources. Establishing program management within the organization is another option. The program manager oversees multiple projects, with the ability to coordinate resources, costs, schedules, and benefits across projects and to align projects with the strategic goal(s) of the organization. Program management can also include the management and assignment of the project managers within the organization. The PMO and the program manager can work to decrease internal competitiveness, providing better use of resources and efficiencies for the organization.

Culture of the Virtual Nomad

According to Garton and Wegryn [35], being a virtual employee means you are working together, apart; it does not mean you are working alone. Some employees, however, may prefer to think otherwise and work together but alone. The growing number of *virtual nomads* presents a co-culture within organizations that needs to be recognized and understood. Virtual nomads are entrepreneurs and professionals that work regardless of physical location and time zones. They are also called *digital nomads* (digimads), *technomads*, or *mobile bohemians* (mobos). Digimads usually have no permanent physical home and earn their income through working on the Internet. Technomads, similar to digimads, are individuals working virtually using the Internet as the main communication source, traveling more often than not. The mobo is not necessarily nomadic but considered spontaneous and more involved with social interaction using portable devices in addition to any work-related interaction. Virtual nomads have also been called *cosmopolitans*—individuals who have lived in several countries, speak multiple languages, and have a global worldview.

Using technology, nomads value location independence, meaning that they choose to work from wherever they wish, regardless of time zone issues with the rest of their team. This nomad existence enables a lifestyle of physical independence while earning an income. Often virtual nomads will work from beaches, cafes, or boats and move from location to location around the world. The true virtual nomad is not concerned with the advantages of stationary life, such as health care providers, grocery stores, banks, and other conveniences. Instead, they do online banking, find food and necessities wherever they are located using a global positioning system (GPS), and use local urgent care or walk-in doctors for health services. They pride themselves on the ability to be resourceful and adaptable, while maintaining a work schedule and producing deliverables for their organization or clients. As long as they can connect to the Internet, the virtual nomad prefers to work wherever is convenient for him or her. Virtual nomads remain connected through communications media during travel and while at different locations. Unconstrained by location and freed from an office, the virtual nomad is able to interact, connect, work, access information, multitask, and stay updated on project work while roaming unencumbered by time and space [36]. Like nomadic ancestors from older cultures in the world, they believe wandering to be a natural stage for human beings and that human curiosity is a motivating attribute for their lack of dependence upon a geographic location [37]. The online nomadic lifestyle is a new co-culture in organizations and a growing choice of many individuals on virtual teams.

Another aspect of nomadic life in organizations is the current trend toward cubicle-free offices. Some organizations are opting for office space with zero cubicles and offices in an attempt to foster leaner and more agile work environments [38]. The open, flexible facilities require that employees gather around tables or in conference rooms to work. The employee has no assigned desk or permanent cubicle and must carry a laptop computer, cell phone, wireless telephone headsets, other electronic devices, and any supplies needed to work. Filing cabinets are often on wheels and pushed to the location of a meeting. All team members sit together and share table space and chairs as needed. Those trumpeting this environment posit that it eliminates the issues of ego and hierarchy and supports teamwork, collaboration, productivity, and efficiency [39]. Examples of organizations with zero cubicles are SAP's Palo Alto campus, Intel, Microsoft Asia Pacific, and Oticon. Oticon states that the cubicle-free environment has helped with retention of employees [40]. Wireless technology and the expenses of office furniture, phones, and office space have caused some organizations to try cubicle-free offices for financial reasons. The result is a virtual, nomadic employee within the confines of an office building—whether that employee chooses the nomadic style or not. The company's identity and culture need to support this in-house nomadic work style. There should be a definite need to fulfill the company's financial, strategic, and functional requirements and productivity using the nomadic environment. Unlike the true virtual nomad, the majority of these in-house nomads have not chosen this work environment. Leading these workers requires a good understanding of virtual work because many of the issues are the same. In addition, complicated challenges such as dealing with workplace tensions, dehumanization, noise, privacy issues, and the feeling many workers have of being "disposable" must be overcome by management.

INTEGRATING ORGANIZATIONAL AND NATIONAL CULTURES

Integrating Cultures

Quoting from Wharton [41]: "Working across international, cultural and organizational boundaries poses daunting challenges on a variety of levels." Diversity—multinational, multicultural, and within the organization—does pose many issues and challenges but can also represent new opportunities. Successful integration of national cultures into one strong organizational culture can be an advantage in the competitive global marketplace. Ample evidence supports the fact that integrating organizational and national cultures is necessary for organizational effectiveness in the 21st century [42].

The influence of national cultures can be difficult for any organization to overcome [43]. National culture influences employees more than organizational culture, and the challenge is for international companies to understand and blend various national cultures into their organization's culture. Executives surveyed on the challenges of global organizations stated obtaining a common corporate culture and identity as a major barrier to successful integration [44]. The organization's norms, standards, values, and behaviors need to be acceptable to all individuals within the organization, regardless of location, ethnic background, or nationality. Differences in perception, status, interpreting context, and communication patterns must be either blended or accepted to be successful. It is critical not only to understand cultural differences but to know when and if to accept them. A virtual project manager (anonymous) currently working with multicultural teams within an organization sums it up this way: "It is a big mistake to try to change your global partners to bridge the cultural gap. You will be wasting your time. You have to respect that it exists and you have to adjust your style to work with them. It will be worth it—believe me. Not understanding their ways will result in an unsuccessful project. You have to be sensitive to their concept of time, religion, power, communication, and individualism."

National and organizational cultural differences can affect employee interactions, communications, and knowledge sharing [45], thus compromising the strength of the organization. Cultural differences may also affect the organization's ability to process information (especially if multiple languages are involved), distort perceptions, and influence behaviors [46]. Confounding the challenges to integrating international and organizational cultures are differences in management styles, differences in metric specifications, legal structures, motivators, contract negotiation and contract understanding, and leadership training. Differences in cultures can contribute to strained interpersonal relationships and inconsistencies between management philosophies. Too many leaders in multinational organizations "retain many of their original national values despite routinely working in culturally diverse situations," and 50% of the differences in managers' attitudes, beliefs, and values are based on national cultural differences [47].

Some organizations opt to assemble virtual teams according to complementary cultures. Grouping culture clusters based upon the primary dimensions of culture (individualism/collectivism, power distribution, uncertainty avoidance, masculinity versus femininity, monochronic/polychronic, and context) can eliminate some cultural challenges. Teams that have a good cultural "fit" while still being multicultural can seem like an attractive solution to some of the multicultural challenges of global teams. Homogeneous teams may have the advantages of high productivity and efficiency because of the team members' similarities. In addition, the homogeneous team in the virtual environment may encourage equality between the team members and promote participation. However, inclusiveness is an organizational training and development opportunity, and firms that train virtual and collocated employees on intercultural awareness may have the advantage in the 21st century. Grouping culture clusters while working in a global business environment may develop homogeneous teams that eventually stagnate the organization and lead to decisions made by the group that discourage creative ideas and encourage anonymity ("groupthink"). The lack of diversity in a team may also inhibit information sharing outside of the group, causing exclusion of individuals and their ideas, expertise, and knowledge.

Leading the Integrated Culture

Acculturation is defined as "the process by which individuals change both by being influenced by contact with another culture and by being participants in the general acculturative change underway in their own culture" [48]. The leader of the integrated culture should understand and convey the value of retaining cultural identity and diverse characteristics to the integrated group—clearly defining and identifying the importance of the integrated culture while also balancing the retention of important cultural concepts from the integrated individuals [49]. Leadership should determine which specific elements of the blended cultures will be encouraged and continued in the new culture, with the input of individuals from all cultures being assimilated. When leadership clearly defines a new culture, integration will most likely be successful and stress levels lower [50].

Acculturation stress, or the lack of cultural integration and recognition of cultural diversity, can lead to serious problems within the organization. The process of acculturation, when not handled correctly, can lead to absenteeism, voluntary turnover in the organization, and a lowering of self-esteem in the individuals within the organization [51]. Substance abuse, depression, and fatigue are also indicators of acculturation stress. Leadership has a responsibility to develop a positive organizational culture and to encourage successful acculturation. An integrated culture should promote higher self-esteem for the individuals, hope, trust, optimism, and flexibility [52]. The leader can work toward successful acculturation by recognizing that acceptance of the new, or second, culture involves changes at both the individual and group levels. Leaders that recognize the importance of the individual while focusing on the emergence of the new culture can enable the integration of different cultural management practices in the new organization [53]. Cultural diversity can be a source of synergy and innovation when organizations adopt a multinational strategy that includes recognition of the benefits of diverse cultures [54].

GLOBALIZATION AND COMMUNICATIONS

The following quote indicates the complexity of globalization and communications: "Overlay cultural behavior and expectations on the roles of communication, team leadership and group dynamics, and you immediately understand. Moreover, there are logistics to overcome: challenges inherent in working in different time zones, lots of travel, and busy conflicting schedules" [55]. Research has shown that global virtual teams face multiple challenges, including communication, culture, technology, and leadership [56]. In addition to these challenges, organizations are often unprepared to make the changes necessary to be successful in the global virtual environment. Many lack training in inclusiveness, necessary for dealing with multiple cultures, and do not have the technology available to provide virtual teams with the tools needed for success. Planning and strategy must be in place prior to the decision to "go global" or "do virtual" for an organization to be competitive. Not all companies are able to do so, nor should all companies.

Barriers to Globalization

Globalization, or the expansion of an organization beyond domestic boundaries, is a strategic decision for a company. Several factors may limit an organization from expanding globally. One of the biggest issues facing a company that hopes to globalize is the ability or inability to localize to "fit" the country it is marketed in without raising production and distribution costs [57]. If the company is unable to do this, then globalization may not be an alternative for them. The global economy is also a factor that may prevent expansion. Fluctuating exchange rates and the costs of labor, distribution, and possibly production can inhibit the move to global enterprise. Companies with little or no profit margin are at high risk when moving into global markets [58].

If the company is highly local (an example would be a company involved in lawn care products), it may not be adaptable to global expansion (such as producers of elevators or cameras) [59]. Foreign countries that have little or no presence of similar competing products may be unsuccessful markets. The ability to globalize also requires the ability to understand the needs of the customer. To move into a global position in an area that does not need the product or service shows a lack of strategic planning on the part of the organization. No amount of virtual communication or project work can change the fact that the organization does not fit the needs of the chosen country. The degree of vertical integration already in place in the organization, backward or forward, may decrease the number of economies of global marketing [60]. In addition, the lack of foreign strategic partnerships, joint ventures, and alliances may prohibit international growth [61]. Domestic and foreign regulations may prohibit entrance into the global market. This would be applicable to banking, insurance, and other highly regulated industries. Some industries may face expensive foreign barriers, such as licensing, that may make services and products noncompetitive in the global market.

Lack of understanding of foreign customer preferences and business and country cultures and lack of international management experience are reasons why an organization should not consider expanding globally. Working on global project management teams requires an understanding of cultural differences, access to the right individuals in each culture represented, and common goals and communication technologies. Organizations need to allocate appropriate technologies to provide the necessary mediums of communication for global project management.

The infrastructure of the organization has to be able to support the communication and technology systems necessary for international communication. In addition, the individuals within the organization need to have training and the ability to use the technology necessary. Global organizations should consider mandatory cross-cultural training in communication, project management, working in multicultural teams, and stakeholder management. There should be guidelines in place and support for project managers, from help in writing charters to selecting communication and collaboration technologies to relationship building and more, to ensure the success of the global project team.

COMMUNICATING ACROSS CULTURES

Cultural Fluency

Culture and communication are linked by the ability to identify, understand, and apply cultural variables, described as *cultural fluency* [62]. Cultural fluency should be a top priority for organizations with multicultural, international virtual projects. Individuals on project teams can represent a mix of different cultures, religions, competencies, ages, genders, and nationalities; and often this diversity can produce more innovations for the organization than a homogeneous team could produce.

Cultural fluency, or the ability to cross cultural boundaries, can be increased by employing good listening skills to notice international differences. Marchetti's [63] advice that listening to and focusing on customers increases effective sales communication can be applied to global project communications. Input from international team members is a major part of a successful global project, but the international partners must be listened to and understood. Language is a major issue in understanding and being understood in global teams. Individuals who speak the same first language may have difficulty understanding team members from different cultures attempting to speak in their language.

Cross-cultural communication interactions that improve cultural fluency include listening, avoiding ambiguity, respecting differences, and understanding without judgment [64]. Cultural sensitivity is one of the top competencies an international virtual project manager can have. As one international project manager (anonymous) says: "I think one of the most important things when working with diverse teams is to realize that not everyone has the same cultural background, and this may impact how they act, interact, and react. This doesn't mean you have to know every culture around the world, but you do need to have this awareness." This type of mindfulness regarding cultural awareness is essential to communicating with cultural fluency.

Training in cultural fluency is important in global organizations. Cultural competence, or the knowledge and understanding about other races, ethnic groups, cultures, and minority groups, can be taught in the classroom or online. The project manager can incorporate team building exercises, formal training, or coaching as a strategy to improve cultural fluency among the team members. Included in this training should be the legal issues that surround diversity. Discrimination on the basis of race, ethnic background, religion, age, gender, and physical disability, for example, is illegal in the United States. Developing cultural fluency means not only embracing cultural diversity but also understanding the law. For the global leader or project manager, cultural fluency can also be accomplished through studying other cultures and customs, language immersion classes, traveling to other countries, participating in community activities, and socially seeking out individuals who are different.

Use of Language and Words

Language is a social behavior, dependent upon where and how an individual was raised [65] and reflects what is important to the individuals in a specific culture. Often managers from the United States use words in international situations that cause international project members to think they are being judged—even if no bad intentions are meant. Terms such as *third world, working-class poor, undeveloped nations*, and terms that include the words *right* or *correct* often cause others to think of judgments, not descriptions. To avoid bias in communication, terms should be as specific as possible about the culture being described. For example, Asian could be specifically stated as Korean; Native American as the tribal name, such as Hopi; or Hispanic as Cuban American. Correct terms encourage cultural understanding and acceptance. Cultural awareness and buy-in are essential to global operations, and words indicate various reflections of how different cultures view what is said.

The use of the pronouns in verbal and written communications can do much to develop trust and relationships in the multicultural team. *I,*

Individualistic   Collectivistic

FIGURE 4.8
Using collectivistic terms in communications.

me, and *you* are individualistic in orientation. The pronouns *we*, *our*, and *us* reflect a more collectivist and plural voice. The use of *I*, *me*, and *you* may indicate ambition and control to those from collectivistic cultures (Figure 4.8).

A direct, low-context way of saying no may be an acceptable way of expressing an opinion in North America, but not in collectivist or high-context cultures. These cultures might express disapproval by saying yes. The Chinese, a collectivistic culture, will use yes or no to express the respect for the feelings of others—saying yes because it is what they feel the listener wants to hear. In Japan, yes often means simply, "Yes, I am listening to you," not, "I agree." Cultural differences in words that are meant to be positive can also be misinterpreted. For example, the project manager who recommends a team player as *ambitious* may be wishing to compliment that individual—but the meaning in another culture may be that this individual was overly political, did not respect authority, or did not work well with the team. When these challenges arise in the team, the e-leader needs to encourage listening skills or, if necessary, lead the team toward agreement on what is acceptable as terms of agreement and recognition. Some organizations provide their global project managers with a dictionary of right and wrong terms to use in multicultural communications. If the project team is having difficulty with word usage, a similar dictionary of terms might be helpful.

Jargon and slang produce miscommunication and confusion in virtual teams. Even teams that speak the same language can become frustrated over words and phrases that do not mean the same thing to different co-cultures or in geographic regions—despite the same language and country.

In multicultural teams that have individuals with multiple languages involved, phrases such as "I'll keep you in the loop" may mean nothing to the team member with English as a second language. References such as "Better eat your spinach!" are missing the contextual background of the Popeye cartoons and mean nothing to the person who has never been exposed to this culturally based cartoon character. Acronyms should be avoided in multicultural teams. The first time an acronym is used, spell the word out completely. Then place the acronym beside the word in parentheses. After that, the acronym can then be used. If the document is long, it is recommended that this process be repeated for each new paragraph, section, or chapter of the communication. Table 4.5 provides an example of the proper use of acronyms when communicating with multicultural teams.

The project manager needs to be a good listener and reader, watching carefully for any use of language or words that might cause potential miscommunication among the members of the multicultural team. In addition, the virtual project manager should carefully select the correct language and wording in all communications. As one experienced virtual project manager says (anonymous): "Depends a lot on the culture. For Americans where I have no language barriers, I can frequently use a 'dump and run' method where I explain in person, give an example, and off I go. For Japanese, I have to be very aware of the words I am using, keep my sentences short and words simple. Same is true for Vietnam, France, Austria, Croatia: I always try to speak to my remote teams as if I were talking to a six-year-old. Not in any way condescending, but in a way to ensure clarity and direction, and to make sure that they are not afraid to ask me any questions. I have found that Asian cultures are very reluctant to ask questions and also to say no to impossible requests."

TABLE 4.5

Using Acronyms in Multicultural Communications

When?	How?
First use	The Illinois Department of Transportation (IDOT) has suggested that we …
Second use—same paragraph, section, or chapter	After we have implemented the IDOT suggestions …
Extended text—new paragraph, section, or chapter	Again, we must complete all the Illinois Department of Transportation (IDOT) recommendations before we can …

Communicating across Time Zones

Virtual teams must communicate with members that are located in multiple time zones. These time zones often cross day and night lines and sometimes even cross date lines. An e-leader may e-mail the team in the afternoon but team members may not receive the e-mail until the next morning. If those team members e-mail back to the e-leader in the afternoon, the leader may not read the e-mail until the next morning. This is a potential delay of one day to send and receive information. Time lost is money lost in business, and dealing with time zones is a major issue in the global environment. Time zone information can be found on the Internet at www.worldtimezone. com, www.timeanddate.com, and http://24timezones.com/. These websites can be very helpful in displaying time by world, region, country, and even internationally by city name. Several provide time zone converters. Many computers provide a desktop accessory clock that has access to time zone information and will convert time.

When setting guidelines for time zones for a virtual team, it is important to recognize Coordinated Universal Time (UTC). UTC follows the International Atomic Time (TAI) with an exact offset of an integer number of seconds, changing only when a leap second is added to keep clock time synchronized with the rotation of the earth. UTC was previously called Greenwich Mean Time (GMT) and UTC is sometimes written informally as GMT. Time zones around the world are expressed as positive or negative offsets from UTC. Many Internet and World Wide Web standards, computer servers, online services, flight plans and air traffic control, weather forecasts and maps, and radio operators use UTC to avoid confusion with time zones and daylight savings time.

The project manager can consider consolidating the virtual team member resource list into major time regions. Using three to four major regions, such as the following, the e-leader can quickly identify the individuals in a region, which is helpful when dealing with multiple time zones [66]:

- North America, Latin America, Caribbean
- Europe, Middle East, Africa
- Asia Pacific
- Collocated (same place, same time zone)

Determining major time regions is helpful when finding the best times for conference calls and NetMeetings. It can also help to ensure that information from one shift gets to the other shift for reviews and hand-offs. A simple solution to a 10½- to 13½-hour time difference is to have some team members stay later while others arrive earlier and rotate these roles on a regular basis.

A best practice for virtual project managers is to develop a Team Member Time Zone spreadsheet at the beginning of the project. The spreadsheet is developed from the time perspective of the project manager and details the information for each team member from that time perspective. When scheduling meetings or attempting to reach a specific team member, the spreadsheet becomes a useful tool. The Time Zone Converter—Time Difference Calculator and the World Clock Meeting Planner at http://www.timeanddate.com/worldclock/converter.html make this one-time set up easy. Figure 4.9 shows some of the information that can be stored on the project manager's Team Member Time Zone spreadsheet.

It is important to note the earliest and latest times that the team member can be contacted. Also important is to note the days of the week. What might be the project manager's Friday could very well be the team member's Saturday. Country alone is not enough for the spreadsheet—city should also be used, as time zones can be different throughout a country. Some project managers include more information on the spreadsheet: role, e-mail, work phone, cell, fax, address, best time to call, and preferred form of correspondence [67]. When building a spreadsheet with this much detail, organization is the key. An example of how a Team Member Information Spreadsheet might be prepared is demonstrated in Figure 4.10. Note that religious preference is included in this spreadsheet. Often holidays are linked to religious dates, and these must be considered in multicultural communications.

When communications occur is the responsibility of the e-leader for the project. The process of providing effective communications for the global multicultural project team is a major factor in developing trust within the team. Setting simple standards, such as "All meetings will be scheduled at central standard time," become important to the success of the project team. Techniques such as beginning meetings by asking what time it is for everyone involved and changing meeting dates frequently so everyone has a chance to participate at the most convenient time are helpful to developing trust and a positive relationship on the international team [68]. All members of the team should have information regarding when and how to contact each other as part of the communications plan for the project.

Name	City	Country	Time Zone	Time Difference +/-	UTC* Offset	Meetings No Earlier Than	Meetings No Later Than	Days of Week

FIGURE 4.9

Project manager's team member time zone spreadsheet.

* Coordinated Universal Time

Name	
Role	Time zone
City	Time difference +/–
Country	UTC* offset
e-Mail	Meetings no earlier than
Work phone	Meetings no later than
Cell phone	Days of week
Fax	Preferred form of communication
Religious preference	Holidays

FIGURE 4.10
Team member information spreadsheet.
* Coordinated Universal Time

Deadlines and Urgency Issues

The Hopi Indians of Arizona make no distinction in their language between past, present, and future tenses. Their perception of time, therefore, is very different from many other cultures. In France, 5 p.m. is often considered the end of the day. Timeliness is viewed as approximate in Brazil and Argentina, so leaving early in the afternoon on a warm and sunny day is not unusual. An afternoon siesta might be totally acceptable in Latin America. Being right on time might be considered rude in Latin America or Turkey. These are examples of polychronic cultures. But being late for a meeting in New York or Berlin would be considered rude and an insult to the individuals attending the meeting. It would indicate that the latecomer does not value the time of the other team members and is an example of a monochronic culture.

Many cultures vary in their understanding of urgency and deadlines. In some collectivistic cultures, everyone on the team might stay at work and maintain a united front for one team member until the entire team's work is completed [69]. In an individualistic culture, the other team members might quit work at 5 p.m. and leave the remaining team member alone to work late. Formal cultures tend to understand the importance of timelines and deadlines more quickly and easily than informal cultures. The team member from an informal, polychronic culture may place less emphasis on scheduling, timetables, milestone dates, and deadlines. Their perspective may be more long-term. In some countries a deadline of several months may be reasonable, but in others a reasonable deadline for the same project may be a few weeks. Such differences have definite consequences to the project in measurable, tangible costs. They also have definite consequences to the project team in trust, relationship, and communications. The e-leader needs to set specific guidelines regarding deadlines and urgency issues. Clear rules concerning meeting times, length of meetings, and agenda items should be set early during the planning process and communicated to all the team members.

Age Discrimination as Cultural Awareness

In the United States the average life expectancy has more than doubled since 1776, from 35 years to 75–86 years for men and to 83–91.5 years for women [70]. Although the Age Discrimination in Employment Act (ADEA) in the United States has been in effect since 1967 and was amended in 1978 and 1986, age still remains an issue in the workplace [71].

Each age group represents individuals with a cultural tendency that can bring heterogeneity to the team, both in a positive or negative manner [72]. A project team with a mix of individuals by age and gender increases the diversity of ideas and experiences to enrich the project but may also create difficulties in communication, interpersonal relationships, and problem solving within the team. Common issues related to age differences in teams are time spent in meetings, pace of work, workloads, and contribution. Global issues arise around younger managers from low-power distance cultures working with senior management from high-power distance cultures. These issues usually arise when senior managers from high-power distance cultures are required to report to younger, lower ranked team members. Often the project manager must intervene to show respect where perceived violations have occurred. The challenge for the project manager is how to maintain an age-neutral workforce (one in which age is not the issue, but the quality of employee and work is) in the current business environment. Suggestions include ongoing management training on age-related issues, engaging the entire team in strategy planning, ensuring inclusive social networking activities, recruiting team members for competencies, and matching older (bringing experience) and younger (bringing energy) employees on teams [73].

Religious Considerations in the Multicultural Team

One of the protections enacted by Title VII of the Civil Rights Act of 1964 in the United States was protection from discrimination on the basis of religion [74]. Religion has become an increasing challenge in the work place, just as it has become in the worldwide political and social arenas. The challenge of religious diversity can have a positive impact for an organization. The acceptance of different religions brings with it the diversity of philosophical thought and resulting creativity. Tolerance of religious practices, from Muslim employees practicing their daily prayers during scheduled breaks to Bible study groups over the lunch hour to openly expressive religious workers [75], allows for inclusion in the organization and promotes more engaged employees. Multicultural organizations should include religion in their antiharassment policy and train management to respond appropriately to requests for religious accommodations. A spiritually open multicultural project team can accept and honor religious practices without compromising the rights of others by implementing the same guidelines and expectations as the organization's mission statement or code of conduct in the project plan. Many organizations post religious holiday calendars and the organization's policies on their websites. Examples include Grinnell University, at http://www.grinnell.edu/offices/studentaffairs/chaplain/calendar, and Binghamton University, at http://www2.binghamton.edu/multicultural-resource-center/docs/holidays-observances-2012.pdf. A complete calendar of religious holidays can be found at InterfaithCalendar.org and is an excellent resource when developing a work schedule for multicultural projects.

Resentment over observing religious practices, such as missing work on Fridays due to prayer requirements, can undermine the trust and relationships in multicultural teams. The e-leader should be sensitive to any indication that someone on the team, or the entire team, may be blaming the source of a problem on religious customs and practices. One of the best responses for religious resentment is the creation of official policies regarding these differences by the organization, inclusion of these policies in the project procedures and documentation, and training by the organization for all employees on these policies [76].

Second Language Concerns

Often multicultural teams include individuals with several different languages and this can make communications challenging and difficult.

One virtual team member expressed frustration over second language concerns this way (anonymous): "In the new world of business globalization, the company I work for started to award engineering contracts to an Indian engineering firm to save money. When the engineers came to our site for a meeting I could only understand about 25% of what they were saying. My job at the time was to work directly with the electrical engineers providing site standard information and system design preferences. Our daily interactions were so uncomfortable because I would have to ask them to repeat their words over and over as I struggled to comprehend what they were trying to say. I'm not sure how much my employer is saving but I'm afraid the huge communication gap is going to result in a miscommunication that will negate all savings."

Preference by the organization and the project manager for their first language may cause unfairness in practice. More fluent team members may get the credit for work simply because they are able to better articulate their thoughts in meetings [77]. Accents can lead to discrimination if not managed properly. For example, an individual with a British accent may get a more prominent task because he or she "sounds better" or "smarter" than an individual with English as a second language. Lack of fluency in a particular language should not be equated with lack of intelligence. This type of language discrimination can also be seen within countries. An individual with a certain dialect may improperly indicate more education (for example, a Massachusetts or East Coast accent) than another accent (for example, an accent of someone from Georgia or the deep south of the United States). When these issues arise in the team, the project manager needs to be sure to assign work according to principles that are fair and accurate, and help coach the team and individual team members in understanding that lack of language fluency does not indicate incompetence. Early in the project, expectations and norms should be set around language fluency that encourage team members to ask for clarification if they cannot understand someone, instead of pretending that they understand or resenting the fact that they cannot understand. Management intervention to remind the team of the qualifications required to be on the team can be helpful. Providing the team with dialect training has not proven to be as successful as setting expectations and management intervention [78].

FLEXIBILITY IN COMMUNICATING
WITH MULTICULTURAL TEAMS

The following quotes were taken from interviews with virtual project managers (anonymous):

> The style you choose in one culture may not produce results in another. A project manager must be cognizant of this when managing virtual teams. You just need to be more cognizant of differences in culture, language, geography, and have to compensate for the limited face-to-face interaction by, for example, having more frequent status meetings.

> Since every team has different needs for direction based on the language, culture, experience level, it is necessary to adapt the management style to get the most from the team. For example, in a culture where deadlines and dates are not a firm commitment, it is key to emphasize the dates. In a culture where bad news is frowned upon, it is necessary to monitor closely for any issues that may not be reported on, and ensure that there will be no surprises at the end.

> Adaptive communication methods are very important—some people prefer e-mail, some phone, and some in-person. With virtual teams, videoconference, phone, and e-mail are sometimes the only options, so a project manager should be prepared to use all of them.

> You must know the cultures and the teams. Each one requires a unique leadership style. Different language or regional cultural differences can impact your project. You should adapt your style to what works best for the team members. You have to change your own behavior to get the best out of your staff in India, but that behavior has to change radically to get the best out of the staff in South Korea.

All these experienced managers project the same concept regarding dealing with multicultural team communications—multiple cultures require multiple leadership styles. Flexibility and situational leadership techniques are important to the success of the team and the project. The amount and type of communication and leadership are dependent upon the team's needs. Because there is often little or no opportunity to meet face-to-face with global teams, the e-leader must be able to communicate with individuals from all cultures regardless of their cultural dimension. As the project evolves, multiple leadership styles may be necessary, just as multiple communications styles may be necessary. Adding to that are multicultural communication needs and styles, making the project manager even more of a chameleon in the role of e-leader. Working across international, organizational, and cultural boundaries involves juggling multiple challenges—cultural fluency, language barriers, time zones, differences in cultural perceptions of deadlines and urgency, age and religious discrimination, and dealing with second language issues. In addition, less obvious diversity issues can cause problems with global teams. The unspoken multicultural issues lying beneath the surface may emerge without notice. The virtual project manager must be able to respond to each challenge, dependent upon the situation, the team, and the individual, to provide the best e-leadership for the global organization.

LOOKING AHEAD: E-LEADERSHIP COMPETENCIES

The project manager of the multicultural project should be aware of any personal biases, be open to different ways of doing things, and participate in cultural training to develop the competencies necessary to lead a multicultural team. Communication competencies are vital to the success of the project. The virtual project manager, however, needs a multitude of competencies to be successful leading the global, multicultural team. Chapter 5 will explore some of the major competencies necessary to be a successful e-leader.

Case Study 4.1: In the Dark

[As told to the author by "Ann," from a large U.S.-based financial organization (anonymous interview)]

OVERVIEW

When you get into other cultures, like in India, people don't want to fail. So they don't necessarily tell you, "Oh, we are having difficulties doing this." They'll just not show up for meetings, and you are thinking, "Are these people sleeping on me?" It's just such a cultural difference that if you set the expectations and put the team at ease from the beginning—I mean it's still difficult dealing with different time zones and if they have questions it's midnight my time. You know, it's hard for them to just talk to people at the beginning of the day or the end of the day because it's about 12 hours' difference. So with setting those expectations, like if you are having trouble or getting into these situations—here are the rules of the road—you need to send an e-mail. And if you set those things up ahead of time, then you can go to whoever is leading their team out there and go back to them and say, "Here's what's working on the team and here's what's not. You know, we're still getting some of your people to call us and tell us that they are not ready, but there's more potential." You have to get to know their leaders and you have to develop relationships. These are virtual teams. They are not robots—they are human beings. And if they aren't getting their questions answered, then how can we perform as a team? If we're doing something and they aren't getting the information that they need, then we need to set up a dialog. You don't have the opportunity to be face-to-face, like when people sit in a conference room and work things out. That doesn't work for virtual teams. You've got to leave the egos at the door or you will shut people down and you won't get anything out of them. You can call them, you can Skype them, you can e-mail them, and they will just put you off, so you really have to make sure that you're their go-to person. You want people to be comfortable talking to you or you need to develop relationships with their managers so they can let you know what's going on with the team, or otherwise, you're in the dark.

DEBRIEF

This project manager outlines the differences between the cultures immediately in the conversation. Ann says, "When you get into other cultures, like in India, people don't want to fail." This comment indicates a culture with high uncertainty avoidance. Individuals with high uncertainty avoidance tend to stay in situations that are familiar, take few risks, and fear failure. She continues by saying, "So they don't necessarily tell you, 'Oh, we are having difficulties doing this,'" and later states, "You can call them, you can Skype them, you can e-mail them, and they will just put you off." The inability of the team members to speak out and state the problem is a direct indication of high-context culture. In a high-context culture, individuals speak in an indirect, ambiguous, and inexplicit manner, causing a reluctance to speak negatively, say no, or explain that they are having trouble with something. Ann has the feeling that when she hangs up from the conference call, she never knows what they really think. The team from India is extremely polite and subservient. "They'll just not show up for meetings," Ann continues, again emphasizing the high-context culture of the team members from India. She understands that India is a high-context culture, so the team members are not likely to speak out and communicate directly. The team members from India are more ambiguous and relationship oriented than her other team members from low-context cultures.

Ann has taken a positive approach to managing her multicultural virtual team. She states, "If you set the expectations and put the team at ease from the beginning," and, "So with setting those expectations, like if you are having trouble or getting into these situations, here are the rules of the road." She also says, "if you set those things up ahead of time." Setting clear expectations, the virtual project manager needs to outline and define the expectations that are appropriate for communications and the participation expected.

In addition, the team from India is very status conscious, and almost a high-power distance culture when interacting with the rest of her multicultural team. She handles this challenge by working with their supervisor when necessary, someone who can talk with them face-to-face regarding performance issues, because she is unable to travel to India herself. This allows the team member to save face in front of the rest of the team, project manager, and the supervisor. We hear this when Ann says, "Then you can go to whoever is leading their team out there and go back to them and say, 'Here's what's working on the team and here's what's not. You know, we're still getting some of your people to call us and tell us that they are not ready, but there's more potential.' You have to get to know their leaders and you have to develop relationships." We also hear this when she says, "You want people to be comfortable talking to you or you need to develop relationships with their managers so they can let you know what's going on with the team, or otherwise, you're in the dark."

Ann is convinced that she will not be in the dark with this team.

Case Study 4.2: On the Beach

SCENARIO

Ira adjusted her laptop's screen. The setting sun was hitting it now and she could no longer see her work. It had been a long day, but looking out over the beach made her feel much better about the time she had put into managing the project today. She wiggled her toes deeper into the sand, realizing that tomorrow she would be on a plane to northern Wisconsin—just in time for the predicted snow—for some of the best skiing of the season. She reflected over the problems solved and decisions made with her project team today. It was hard to be patient with two of them this morning—but, Ira surmised, patience and persistence would pay off in the long run. It always did with these start-up projects. Ira checked her GPS to find a good local restaurant for dinner. Last night's dining "opportunity" hadn't been very good, and she was eager to have her last night on the island a dinner that used local foods and recipes. She messaged Varya saying that she was heading out for dinner and calling it a day. Varya, one of her team leaders, was in a different time zone and would continue to handle any issues overnight. She closed her laptop. Her virtual project team would have to wait two hours—she was taking off for dinner. But first, she leaned back in her chaise lounge and watched the sun set.

DEBRIEF QUESTIONS

1. What type of leadership style does Ira represent in this scenario?
2. Can a project manager be a virtual nomad?
3. How can Ira's immersion in different cultures contribute to her cultural fluency?
4. How is Ira using multiple time zones to her advantage on the virtual project?

Case Study 4.3: It's Not That Funny

[As told to the author by "A," from a large U.S.-based financial organization (anonymous interview)]

OVERVIEW

You have to watch humor, too, because people in other cultures—I've worked with people from the Ukrane, Russia, India, not Costa Rica yet—what we think is a joke may not be a joke to somebody else. So there's all these things you have to be knowledgeable about and you need to be able to gauge and understand. You have to understand the culture. Read, connect with the world, use a community of practice, learn about other religions and cultures.

DEBRIEF

"Humor is in the ear of the beholder"—or so a similar saying goes. Here the virtual project manager states, "What we think is a joke may not be a joke to somebody else." For individuals from other cultures, understanding the colloquial nuances of a "joke" may be confounded by the level and tone of the voice of the jokester. Loudness of voice is often associated with telling jokes. Individuals from Latin American, Middle Eastern, and Mediterranean countries speak noticeably louder than other cultures. The result may be that the exchange is simply considered annoying, ignored, or misinterpreted. The project manager has the responsibility to follow up after jokes or humor is used in the multicultural team by saying something like, "Thanks for sharing that joke, Bob." For those on the team with language issues, a simple statement such as this can provide all the translation needed for them to understand that what they heard was humorous and not to be considered otherwise. If someone from the team is telling jokes or using humor that could be considered offensive to another culture, the project manager should talk privately with the individual or provide training in multicultural awareness so the negative behavior does not continue.

Be careful when involving team members in informal, social chit chat. Multicultural team members may find sharing information about personal or family matters offensive and out of place in the business environment [1]. Social conversations and community-building activities can be agreed upon by the team when conducting the team culture discussion early in the project.

NOTES

Anonymous quotes from virtual project managers are taken from survey responses in:

Lee, M. R. (2011). *e-Leadership for project managers: A study of situational leadership and virtual project success.* ProQuest, UMI Dissertation Publishing.

Anonymous interviews:

Lee, M. R. (2013). Interview by M. R. Lee. [Tape recording.] Springfield, IL.

REFERENCES

1. Knowledge@Wharton (2009, September). Locals, cosmopolitans and other keys to creating successful global teams. *University of Pennsylvania.* Retrieved from http://knowledge.wharton.upenn.edu/article.cfm?articleid = 2328.
2. Konrad, A. M. (2006). Leveraging workplace diversity in organizations. *Organizational Management Journal,* 3(3), 164–189 (p. 166).
3. Hofstede, G. (1980, Summer). Motivation, leadership, and organization. Do American theories apply abroad? *Organizational Dynamics,* 9(1), 42–63.
4. Floyd, K. (2011). *Communication matters.* New York: McGraw-Hill.
5. Floyd, K. (2011). *Communication matters.* New York: McGraw-Hill.
6. Hofstede, G. (2003). *Culture's consequences: Comparing values, behaviors, institutions, and organizations across nations* (2nd ed.). Thousand Oaks, CA: Sage.
7. Hofstede, G. (2003). *Culture's consequences: Comparing values, behaviors, institutions, and organizations across nations* (2nd ed.). Thousand Oaks, CA: Sage.
8. Duarte, D., & Snyder, N. (1999). *Mastering virtual teams.* San Francisco: Jossey-Bass.
9. Duarte, D., & Snyder, N. (1999). *Mastering virtual teams.* San Francisco: Jossey-Bass.
10. Floyd, K. (2011). *Communication matters.* New York: McGraw-Hill.
11. Floyd, K. (2011). *Communication matters.* New York: McGraw-Hill.
12. Duarte, D., & Snyder, N. (1999). *Mastering virtual teams.* San Francisco: Jossey-Bass.
13. Duarte, D., & Snyder, N. (1999). *Mastering virtual teams.* San Francisco: Jossey-Bass.
14. Hofstede, G. (2003). *Culture's consequences: Comparing values, behaviors, institutions, and organizations across nations* (2nd ed.). Thousand Oaks, CA: Sage.
15. Knowledge@Wharton (2009, September). Locals, cosmopolitans and other keys to creating successful global teams. *University of Pennsylvania.* Retrieved from http://knowledge.wharton.upenn.edu/article.cfm?articleid = 2328.
16. Floyd, K. (2011). *Communication matters.* New York: McGraw-Hill.
17. Duarte, D., & Snyder, N. (1999). *Mastering virtual teams.* San Francisco: Jossey-Bass.
18. Capella University. (2005). *Managing and organizing people.* Boston: Prentice Hall Custom Publishing. (p. 485).
19. Nelson, D. L., & Quick, J. C. (1996). *Organizational behavior: The essentials.* St. Paul, MN: West Publishing Company.
20. Kotter, J., & Hesket, J. (1992). *Corporate culture and performance.* New York: Free Press.

21. Gordon, J. R. (1999). *Organizational behavior: A diagnostic approach*. Upper Saddle River, NJ: Prentice Hall.
22. Capella University. (2005). *Managing and organizing people*. Boston: Prentice Hall Custom Publishing.
23. Gordon, J. R. (1999). *Organizational behavior: A diagnostic approach*. Upper Saddle River, NJ: Prentice Hall.
24. Veiga, J., Lubatkin, M., Calori, R., & Very, P. (2000, April). Measuring organizational culture clashes: A two-nation post-hoc analysis of a cultural compatibility index. *Human Relations, 53*(4), 539–557. doi: 10.1177/0018726700534004.
25. Bassi, L., & McMurrer, D. (2007). Maximizing your return on people. *Harvard Business Review, 85*(3), 115–124.
26. Lipnack, J., & Stamps, J. (2010). *Leading virtual teams: Expert solutions to everyday challenges*. Boston: Harvard Business Press.
27. Robbins, S. P. (2005/2005). Organizational behavior (11th ed.). In OM 8004, *Managing and organizing people*. Capella University (pp. 483–516). Boston: Pearson Prentice Hall Custom Publishing (p. 488).
28. Pauleen, D. (2004). *Virtual teams: Projects, protocol and processes*. Hershey, PA: Idea Group, Inc.
29. Duarte, D., & Snyder, N. (1999). *Mastering virtual teams*. San Francisco: Jossey-Bass.
30. Pulley, M. L., Sessa, V. I., Fleenor, J., & Pohlmann, T. (2001). e-Leadership: Separating the reality from the hype. *Leadership in Action—LIA, 21*(4), 3–6.
31. Pauleen, D. (2004). *Virtual teams: Projects, protocol and processes*. Hershey, PA: Idea Group, Inc.
32. Kerzner, H. (2006). *Project management: A systems approach to planning, scheduling, and controlling*. Hoboken, NJ: John Wiley & Sons, Inc.
33. Milosevic, D. Z., & Srivannaboon, S. (2006). A theoretical framework for aligning project management with business strategy. *Project Management Journal, 37*(3), 98–110.
34. Whitley, R. (2006). Project-based firms: New organizational form or variations on a theme? *Industrial and Corporate Change, 15*(1), 77–99.
35. Garton, C., & Wegryn, K. (2006). *Managing without walls*. Lewisville, TX: Mc Press Online, LP.
36. Johnson, J. (2011). The new mobile bohemian. *Going mobo*. Retrieved from http://www.goingmobo.com/the-new-mobile-bohemian/.
37. Makimoto, T., & Manners, D. (1997). *Digital nomad*. Chichester, West Sussex, England: Wiley & Sons.
38. Clark, T. (2012). When does it make sense to kill the cubicle? *Forbes Business*. Retrieved from http://www.forbes.com/sites/sap/2012/05/03/when-does-it-make-sense-to-kill-the-cubicle/.
39. Clark, T. (2012). When does it make sense to kill the cubicle? *Forbes Business*. Retrieved from http://www.forbes.com/sites/sap/2012/05/03/when-does-it-make-sense-to-kill-the-cubicle/.
40. Ewing, J. (2007). No-cubicle culture. *Bloomberg Business Week Magazine*. Retrieved from http://www.businessweek.com/stories/2007-08-19/no-cubicle-culture.
41. Knowledge@Wharton (2009, September). Locals, cosmopolitans and other keys to creating successful global teams. *University of Pennsylvania*. Retrieved from http://knowledge.wharton.upenn.edu/article.cfm?articleid=2328.

42. McLaurin, J. R. (2008). Leader-effectiveness across cultural boundaries: An organizational culture perspective. *Journal of Organizational Culture, Communication and Conflict*, 12(1), 49–69. doi:1774726261.

43. Lee, M. R. (2010). Leading and integrating national cultures into an organizational culture. In F. Columbus (ed.), *Public Leadership*. Hauppauge, NY: Nova Science Publishers, Inc.

44. Bellin, J. B., & Pham, C. T. (2007). Global expansion: Balancing a uniform performance culture with local conditions. *Strategy & Leadership*, 35(6), 44–50. doi:1369380711.

45. Sirmon, D. G., & Lane, P. J. (2004). A model of cultural differences and international alliance performance. *Journal of International Business Studies*, 35(4), 306–319. doi:667611771.

46. Gordon, J. R. (1999). *Organizational behavior: A diagnostic approach*. New Jersey: Prentice Hall.

47. Sirmon, D. G., & Lane, P. J. (2004). A model of cultural differences and international alliance performance. *Journal of International Business Studies*, 35(4), 306–319 (p.309). doi:667611771.

48. Berry, J. W. (1990). Psychology of acculturation. In J. Berman (Ed.), *Cross-cultural perspectives: Nebraska symposium on motivation* (p. 235). Lincoln: University of Nebraska Press.

49. Lee, M. R. (2010). Leading and integrating national cultures into an organizational culture. In F. Columbus (ed.), *Public Leadership*. Hauppauge, NY: Nova Science Publishers, Inc.

50. Berry, J. W. (1990). Psychology of acculturation. In J. Berman (Ed.), *Cross-cultural perspectives: Nebraska symposium on motivation* (p. 235). Lincoln: University of Nebraska Press.

51. Bass, W. S. (2003). The acculturative stress/employee withdrawal relationship. *Dissertation Abstracts International* 64(02), 564 (UMI No. 3081430).

52. Peterlin, J., Penger, S., & Dimovski, V. (2009). Authentic leadership as the promising link between Western and Eastern management practices: The case of Slovenian Company. *International Business & Economics Research Journal*, 8(12), 87–98. doi:1949806161.

53. Peterlin, J., Penger, S., & Dimovski, V. (2009). Authentic leadership as the promising link between Western and Eastern management practices: The case of Slovenian Company. *International Business & Economics Research Journal*, 8(12), 87–98. doi:1949806161.

54. Moorhead, G. & Griffin, R. W. (2004). *Organizational behavior: Managing people and organizations*. Boston: Houghton Mifflin Company.

55. Solomon, C. M. (1995). Global teams: The ultimate collaboration. *Personnel Journal*, 74(9), 50.

56. Kayworth, T., & Leidner, D. (2000). The global virtual manager: A prescription for success. *European Management Journal*, 18(2), 183–194.

57. Thompson, A., Strickland, A., & Gamble, J. (2005). *Crafting and executing strategy: Text and readings* (15th ed.). New York: McGraw-Hill.

58. Thompson, A., Strickland, A., & Gamble, J. (2005). *Crafting and executing strategy: Text and readings* (15th ed.). New York: McGraw-Hill.

59. Kotler, P., & Keller, K. L. (2007). *A framework for marketing management* (3rd ed.). Upper Saddle River, NJ: Prentice-Hall.

60. Kotler, P., & Keller, K. L. (2007). *A framework for marketing management* (3rd ed.). Upper Saddle River, NJ: Prentice-Hall.

61. Thompson, A., Strickland, A., & Gamble, J. (2005). *Crafting and executing strategy: Text and readings* (15th ed.). New York: McGraw-Hill.

62. Scott, J. C. (1999). Developing cultural fluency: The goal of international business communication in the 21st century. *Journal of Education for Business, 74*(3), 140–143.

63. Marchetti, M. (2007). Listen to me! *Sales and Marketing Management, 159*(3), 12.

64. Zofi, Y. S. (2011). *A manager's guide to virtual teams.* New York: AMACOM.

65. Tannen, D. (1995). The power of talk: Who gets heard and why. *Harvard Business Review, 73*(5), 139.

66. Garton, C., & Wegryn, K. (2006). *Managing without walls.* Lewisville, TX: Mc Press Online, LP.

67. Lipnack, J., & Stamps, J. (2010). *Leading virtual teams: Expert solutions to everyday challenges.* Boston: Harvard Business Press.

68. Knowledge@Wharton (2009, September). Locals, cosmopolitans and other keys to creating successful global teams. *University of Pennsylvania.* Retrieved from http://knowledge.wharton.upenn.edu/article.cfm?articleid=2328.

69. Behfar, K., Kern, M., & Brett, J. (2006). Managing challenges in multicultural teams. *Managing Groups and Teams, 9,* 233–262. doi: 10.1016/S1534-0856(06)09010-4.

70. Dychtwald, K., & Flower, J. (1989). *Age wave: The challenges and opportunities of an aging America.* New York: G. P. Putnam's Sons.

71. Kahn, S. C., Brown, B. A., & Zepke, B. E. (1984). *Personnel director's legal guide.* Boston: Warren, Gorham & Lamont.

72. Ely, R., & Thomas, D. (2001). Cultural diversity at work: The effects of diversity perspectives on work group processes and outcomes. *Administrative Science Quarterly, 46,* 229–273.

73. Freeman, L. (2007, November 12). Spotlight on: age diversity. *Personnel Today, 27.* Retrieved from http://www.personneltoday.com/articles/12/11/2007/43189/spotlight-on-age-diversity.htm

74. Kahn, S. C., Brown, B. A., & Zepke, B. E. (1984). *Personnel director's legal guide.* Boston: Warren, Gorham & Lamont.

75. MacGillivray, E. D., Beecher, H. J. M., & Golden, D. (2006). Currents: Legal developments—Roundup of employment-related news. *Global Business & Organizational Excellence, 26*(1), 71–97.

76. Behfar, K., Kern, M., & Brett, J. (2006). Managing challenges in multicultural teams. *Managing Groups and Teams, 9,* 233–262. doi: 10.1016/S1534-0856(06)09010-4.

77. Behfar, K., Kern, M., & Brett, J. (2006). Managing challenges in multicultural teams. *Managing Groups and Teams, 9,* 233–262. doi: 10.1016/S1534-0856(06)09010-4.

78. Behfar, K., Kern, M., & Brett, J. (2006). Managing challenges in multicultural teams. *Managing Groups and Teams, 9,* 233–262. doi: 10.1016/S1534-0856(06)09010-4.

CASE STUDY REFERENCE

1. Lipnack, J., & Stamps, J. (2010). *Leading virtual teams: Expert solutions to everyday challenges.* Boston: Harvard Business Press.

5

Virtual Project Leadership Competencies

COMPETENCIES IN PROJECT MANAGEMENT

The definition of a *competency* is an ability or quality of being adequately or well qualified for a specific task. Competencies are a cluster of related abilities, knowledge, and skills that enable a person to act effectively in a wide variety of situations. The list of competencies necessary for a project manager to be successful is comprehensive and lengthy. Management and interpersonal skills were considered the top skills necessary for team leaders by the Center for Creative Leadership [1]. In their research, they found that the largest percentage of skills that team leaders need are in the category of management skills, which includes organizing, making decisions, and prioritizing work through project management. They found that interpersonal skills, which include communication, listening, and diplomacy, are considered the second highest skill category needed for team leaders. Many of the skills necessary for traditional project management are the same for virtual project management:

- General management
- Resource management
- Communication
- Technical knowledge
- Decision making
- Problem solving
- Administration

The list of interpersonal skills important to working with project teams is itself daunting [2]:

- Leadership
- Team building
- Motivation
- Interpersonal communication
- Influencing
- Political and cultural awareness
- Negotiation
- Trust building
- Conflict management
- Coaching

The e-leader must have all these skills to be successful—plus many others. The virtual project manager needs to be trustworthy and build trust for the team; be an excellent communicator, providing clear vision and project objectives, roles and responsibilities, and expectations for the team members; be able to build team cohesiveness virtually; and be able to motivate individuals to work together to produce quality deliverables.

Virtual Project Management Competencies

The role of the virtual project manager, similar to the traditional project manager, is to move the team toward success. This is done through project management and interpersonal skills. Duarte and Snyder [3] suggest that the most important competency is project management expertise, a competency that is required for traditional and virtual project success. The challenge for the virtual team leader is to manage using these competencies in the virtual environment through electronically mediated interactions. As the nucleus for the virtual team, the e-leader must facilitate communications; establish the team processes; and successfully complete the project on time, in budget, in scope, and with a quality deliverable—with team members that are geographically dispersed and of multiple cultures. Yet, virtual project management "remains one of the little understood and often poorly supported elements in the success of virtual teams" [4]. Critical skills for virtual project managers include the following [5,6]:

- Effective understanding and use of technology
  - Skills include use of technology, currency in technology updates, virtual facilitation experience, understanding and expertise with electronic communications and collaboration technology
- Helping team members work independently and be self-sufficient
  - Can work with team members to develop training and growth needs; can adjust leadership style to individual team members' needs for management, supervision, autonomy, or coaching; encourages team to use reasoning and evidence to make decisions
- Managing performance virtually
  - Skills include being able to develop strategy, set performance objectives, establish measurements for performance, conduct performance reviews, champion team members
- Understanding multiple cultures
  - Competent in understanding the dimensions of cultural differences, able to coordinate cultural differences to the advantage of the project, can communicate with sensitivity to cultural differences, can adjust leadership style to the cultural dimension of the individual
- Eliminating barriers for the team
  - Can act as an advocate for team members and project work, able to communicate the team's value and worth to upper management, builds trust with functional and external stakeholders and managers, develops important networks for project work and team members, evaluates alternative course of action through logic, factual, rational judgment

The move from traditional to virtual project management means the e-leader must be willing to adapt some management-style techniques to the global team's needs. Leadership style becomes more directive, being clearer on roles, responsibilities, and processes. Decision-making techniques must now include an understanding of how team members from different cultures make decisions and being open to trying different decision-making options. Communication remains central to the success of the project but becomes more focused and definitive. Setting clear expectations and providing immediate and frequent feedback now means more than weekly team meetings in the boardroom—it may be instant messaging, daily updates, collaboration databases, or social networking. More focus needs to be concentrated on providing reliable and defined processes that ensure team members are working in an environment that can produce the best results. The list of competencies continues to expand for virtual managers. The virtual project manager needs to be trustworthy and build trust for the team; be an excellent communicator; provide clear vision and project goals, roles and responsibilities, and expectations for the team members; be able to build team cohesiveness virtually; lead by example; delegate work and responsibilities effectively; and be able to motivate individuals to work together to produce quality deliverables.

Virtual team members have expectations for the competencies needed for their e-leaders. Fisher and Fisher [7] suggest that virtual employees have 10 common requests for virtual team managers. Table 5.1 reports the responses from their research that compare the skill or competency desired by the virtual team with the opposite, negative action.

Not only does the virtual project manager juggle the competencies for managing, project management, and virtual project management and the requests and needs of the virtual team, but attention must be paid to relationship building with the supervisors and functional managers of the global team members. These individuals play an important role in the success of the project. They can assess performance in the field and help resolve issues that require face-to-face management. Conversely, they can also become distracters from the virtual work if they are requiring other work or activities from the virtual team member. If the virtual employee is located in a remote office, competence in building rapport with functional managers or supervisors is essential to the success of the project.

Understanding the competencies needed for project management and virtual project management and the interpersonal skills for effective leadership involves self-awareness and training on those competencies that the manager might need to improve. Several competencies are prominent in

TABLE 5.1

Ten Most Common Requests—Competencies Wanted vs. Activities Not Wanted

Ten Most Common Requests for Virtual Team Managers	
1. Coordination—not control	6. Decisiveness—not micromanagement
2. Accessibility—not inaccessibility or omnipresence	7. Honesty—not manipulation
3. The right information at the right time—not information overload	8. Concern for individual development—not distance and apathy
4. Feedback—not unsolicited advice	9. Team building—not isolation
5. Fairness—not favoritism	10. Respect—not paternalism or condescension

Source: Fisher, K., & Fisher, M. (2011). *Manager's guide to virtual teams.* New York: McGraw-Hill.

the discussion of leading virtual projects: focus on vision and project objectives, clarity in developing structure and processes, ability to monitor and control the virtual project work, facilitation of project meetings to increase productivity, and status reporting and ensuring team accountability.

COMPETENCIES FOR LEADING VIRTUAL PROJECTS

Focusing on the Vision of the Project

One characteristic of a successful virtual team is the ability of the members to share the responsibility for seeing the vision of the project and completing the mission of the project. The key stakeholders, sponsor(s), and project manager develop a vision statement or purpose statement for the project work during the early phase of the project, the initiation process group of the project life cycle. Developing the mission statement, also called the project overview statement, can be a powerful team-building experience. A project overview statement should clearly describe the project requirements, customer group(s), and how (in terms of resources and technology) the project team is going to satisfy these needs. It should explain the goal of the project, be short and to the point, and define the final deliverable or outcome [9]. A clearly written project overview statement includes a sentence regarding the problem or opportunity to be solved by the project, the project goal and objectives, and success criteria for the project.

Examples of goal statements that clearly state the project information are as follows:

The Clean and Green Project will develop and deliver a list of suggestions to the village regarding community beautification within three months.

The Tech Team will develop procedures for MMA683 processing within two months that will reduce online usage by 5% without affecting MMA683 value.

The statement gives purpose and direction to the project and must be clear and concise. The project manager can reinforce the statement by inserting it at the beginning of the project meeting agendas and minutes. Team members should be expected to know and understand the vision and purpose of the project and be able to respond to questions regarding the goal(s) of the project.

Clarity of Virtual Structure and Processes

The opportunity to create the structure and establish the standards for managing the virtual team comes early in the planning process. Ensuring that everyone is clear on roles, responsibilities, communication expectations, processes, and the expectations for conduct are essential to the success of the virtual team.

Team Charter

Team structure and processes often involve the virtual team members developing a team charter during the planning phase of the project. Included in this document should be information and instructions on the following:

- The project vision, mission, or goal statement
- Meetings
  - Attendance requirements and consequences for not attending
  - When and how meetings will be scheduled (if not part of the communications plan)
  - Responsibilities for setting up meetings, facilitating meetings, agendas, and minutes
  - Rules of engagement that outline how and when team members speak during meetings
  - Etiquette for audio- and video-conferencing
- Communications
  - Handling phone calls and e-mails, call and e-mail return times
  - Guidelines for texting
  - Availability requirements and posting of availability
  - e-Mail etiquette
  - Consequences for poor communication practices
  - Emergency situation procedures and communication information
- Roles and responsibilities
  - Descriptions of roles and responsibilities for project
  - Performance objectives and expectations for individual and team project work

- Responsibility for team communications regarding updates and progress reports for work
  - Guidelines for meeting project deadlines and milestones
  - Accountability and consequences for missed work
  - Procedures for hand-off of deliverables
  - Backup plan for project work that is negatively impacted
- Technology requirements for project work and communications
- Procedures for requests for resources
- Conflict management procedures
  - First steps
  - Escalation process
  - Measures to prevent conflict from negatively impacting work
- Measures for team success
- Documentation
  - Responsibility for issues and risk logs
  - Decision-making protocol
  - Issue escalation protocol

Charters can take a variety of different shapes and styles. If the organization has a standard team charter or template, that should be used. Figures 5.1 and 5.2 show examples of team charters.

Code of Conduct

Many project teams write a code of conduct with the guidance of the project manager. A team that works together to build a code of conduct will more likely buy in to the concept and the code than a team that is presented a list of rules by the project manager [10]. The code of conduct brings a sense of community and unity to the geographically diverse project team. Ethical codes regulate behavior, which can be especially important in the virtual environment. The virtual project manager can monitor the team's work and bring the team together to review the code if problems arise. The People Capability Maturity Model [11] stresses that teams that understand and are invested with the authority to manage their work, performance, and internal processes and that take the responsibilities for their results can become "empowered workgroups" reaching new standards. A code of conduct gives structure around the goals that such a team would work toward to achieve outstanding performance.

Project Charter		
Project team	Project role	Contact information
Mission statement		
Project commitment statement		
Description of project manager role and responsibilities		
Description of team member role and responsibilities		
Description of project sponsor role and responsibilities		
Performance objectives		
Measures of success		
Scope and boundaries of the team's work		
Deliverables		
Project time frame		
Technology requirements		
Project documentation procedures		
Resource request protocol		
Project meeting protocol		
Conflict management protocol		
Decision-making protocol		
Communications protocol		
Issues escalation protocol		

FIGURE 5.1
Sample team charter #1.

Project Team Charter			
Project Name			
Project Number			
Project Manager			
Project Goal Statement			
Team Member Name	Role	Responsibility	Performance Expectations
Meeting Ground Rules			
Attendance Requirements		Consequences for Not Attending	
Meeting Assignments		Responsible Person	
Setting Up Meetings			
Facilitating Meetings			
Agendas and Minutes			
We agree to the following rules of engagement about how and when team members speak during meetings			
Communications Ground Rules			
Phone calls		Return time	
e-Mails		Return time	
Texting		Expectations	
Availability		Expectations	
We agree to the following rules for communication etiquette			

FIGURE 5.2

Sample team charter #2.   *(continued)*

We agree to the following emergency situation communication procedures	
Type of emergency	Who should be contacted and when

Project Work

We agree to the following guidelines for project work

Missed deadlines		Consequences	
Hand-offs		Consequences	

Technology requirements for this project are

Conflict Management

First Step

Escalation

Interference of project work—prevention

Measures for Success

We agree to the following measures for team success

Project Documentation

Issues Log	Responsible person
Risk Log	Responsible person

☐ All team members participated in the creation of this charter and agree with its content. (Please check.)

FIGURE 5.2 (CONTINUED)
Sample team charter #2.

The code of conduct should include the following information:

- Vision and purpose for the project
- Individuals to whom the code applies
- Team values
- Role responsibilities

- Standards
- Respect
- Fairness
- Honesty
- Grievances procedures
- Consequences for cyberbullying and unethical behaviors
- Escalation procedures

The Project Management Institute provides a Project Management Institute Code of Ethics and Professional Conduct [12] for project managers. The code specifically requires that project managers work in an ethical and professional manner and "comply with laws, regulations, and organizational and professional policies" [13].

Monitoring and Controlling the Virtual Project

During the monitoring and controlling process of the project, the virtual project manager must identify and document any changes to the project and provide the guidance, organization, and coordination to track the work for the entire project. Weekly project status meetings, electronically posted updates, and updated issues and risk logs are essential to the success of the virtual project.

On the global, virtual team, flexibility in steering the project is essential to success. One experienced virtual project manager (anonymous) says it this way: "The style of leadership varies according to the project situation; one size does not fit all. Per my experience, flexibility is the approach toward project steering. Virtual projects require clear communication and status tracking and need to apply situation-specific solutions based on progress. If the project is progressing as per timelines, normal tracking and communication meetings should suffice. In case of delay or crashing, the project manager needs to push the team with control and tight communication/tracking for ensuring the success of the project."

A challenge that many virtual managers experience is managing the virtual team without being able to know or see exactly what is happening at any given time. Overseeing the project cannot be managed the same way as with the traditional, collocated team. With virtual teamwork, often by the time the project manager becomes aware of a problem, it may be too late. When a virtual team member fails to return a phone call or e-mail, it is not possible to walk down the hall to visit about the challenge or stop by his or her office to chat. The e-leader wonders if the team member is actually not available at the time—or if the team member is a virtual nomad or exhibits an entrepreneurial style and prefers to work autonomously—or if the work is not being done because of problems. The virtual project manager must rely on technology alone to monitor and control the project and trust the team members to complete the work required.

The role of the virtual project manager changes throughout the project, often depending upon the stage of the project life cycle. What worked in the initiating and planning processes may not be what is required in the monitoring and controlling process. As another global project manager (anonymous) explains: "For example, during the initiating and planning phases, I acted as coach, where I encouraged the team to build on past successes and apply their knowledge of the tasks to the current project. This was because I knew the team and what they could accomplish. During the monitoring and controlling phases, I spent time supporting and delegating work to the team. In some phases I direct, others I seek solutions, and yet other phases I take backseat. Usually the project is completed in a shorter time frame."

Project Meetings

Monitoring and controlling the project work requires clear expectations and communication regarding project meetings. The virtual project manager needs to provide definite rules regarding attendance at meetings and consequences for not attending, making specific meetings a top priority. Expectations also need to be set for turnaround time on e-mails and phone calls. Prioritizing meetings is helpful to virtual team members and can be communicated to the team in the manner shown in Table 5.2. Each meeting should be designated with the priority level, and every team member should understand the consequences for not attending [14].

Status Reporting and Accountability

An effective status and performance reporting system is essential to the success of the virtual project. According to the project schedule, a system needs to be in place for each team member to responsibly report progress clearly and measurably. Accountability for the virtual team member is no different from accountability for the traditional, collocated team member. The work needs to be completed on time, in scope, and with quality. The project manager should develop mechanisms for accountability at the planning phase of

TABLE 5.2

Prioritizing Meetings

Meeting Priority Level	Expectation—Virtual Team Members	Suggested Communication(s)/ Technology
1	Essential—cannot be delegated, must attend (travel may be required)	Face-to-Face or Videoconference— NetMeeting, Skype, Google Gang, MS Linc
2	Critical—cannot be delegated	Video- or Teleconference—NetMeeting, Skype, Google Gang, GoToMeeting, ChatStage, MS Linc
3	General—can be delegated	Video- or Teleconference—NetMeeting, Skype, Google Gang, GoToMeeting, ChatStage, MS Linc
4	Specific—Do not need to attend unless you are on the agenda. Read the minutes.	Video- or Teleconference—NetMeeting, Skype, Google Gang, GoToMeeting, ChatStage, MS Linc Documents available on collaborative database—e-Room, Google Docs, MS EPM
5	N/A—Do not need to attend.	N/A

the project and continue using thorough quality measurements during the executing, monitoring and controlling, and closing phases of the project.

Often the challenge for the project manager is how to manage accountability in the virtual environment. Clear communications are again one of the best practices for ensuring accountability and help provide clarity for the commitments necessary for the team members. Much of this should be done early in the project, when commitments are made to the project by the virtual team members and their individual managers through the development of the work breakdown structure and the project schedule. Be sure the team understands expectations up front regarding roles, responsibilities, status reports, deadlines, decision-making processes, and authority for the project. The project manager should provide regular updates to the project plan and schedule and should be aware and accountable for monitoring milestones and deadlines for the work. As one virtual project manager (anonymous) states, "I have applied specific approaches to ensure timely delivery by guiding teams with closure interactions where I felt the team might slip on targets. In some of the project deliverables where I felt the team was sure to deliver, team leads were entrusted for deliverables." It is the project manager's responsibility to follow up on any missed deadlines and request regular status reports from the team members. In a virtual team this becomes even more important because of the limitations of not being collocated. When a virtual team member is late or missing deadlines, a one-on-one discussion needs to occur and help should be offered if applicable.

Using a collaborative database for documentation of schedules and progress is essential for the virtual project team. The ability to check their own progress and status and find status updates any time of day or night can help the team members stay accountable and responsible to their own work. Shared calendars and project schedules can be posted on the team website or a database. Weekly status reports should be simple and easy to read. They should include date, status of work, project summary, completed tasks, upcoming tasks, deadlines, and names of those accountable [15]. The status report should be included as a communication objective in the project communications plan. A summary status report (Figure 5.3) is

Summary Status Report

Project Name:		Report Period	
Project Number:		From	To
Project Manager:			

Project Status: ☐ Green ☐ Yellow ☐ Red

Key accomplishments last period:
• List brief 1- or 2-sentence descriptions of what was accomplished in this last period.
– Include important schedule milestones if any occurred in this last period.
– Include any events that significantly reduced risk in the project.
– Include key tasks that closed an issue that was marked "open" in the previous report.

Upcoming tasks for this period:
• List brief 1- or 2-sentence descriptions of what you plan to accomplish this next period.
– Include important schedule milestones if any that will occur in this period.
– Include any upcoming events that will significantly reduce risk in the project.
– Include key tasks that will move an open issue toward closure.
– Include any item you specifically need management's help on–and what actions you need.

Issues:
• List principal open issues.
– Include any item you specifically need management's help on–and what actions you need.
– Identify an owner of the issue–who is driving the resolution.
– Include a task in the "Upcoming tasks for this period" that will move this issue toward closure.
– Don't try to track all project issues in this report. Just list the principal ones along with any progress toward closing them.
– If resolving the issue needs management action, be specific about what action is needed and by when.

FIGURE 5.3
Summary status report.

a good tool because it provides a quick overview of the project on one page, with bullet points for easy reading. This report is also useful for managers who want only a broad overview of the project.

A full status report should delegate tasks and list dates for completion. Progress reports can be as simple as listing the deliverables, team member responsible, and status (what has been completed and what still needs to be completed). Placed in the collaborative database or team website, each team member can take the responsibility for updating the progress report for their specific tasks.

The project manager should also keep a status report to track the processes of the project and the tasks the project manager needs to accomplish for each process (Figure 5.4).

In addition, the project manager or project planner is responsible for the project schedule, providing Gantt charts, program evaluation review technique (PERT) analyses, and watching the critical path for the project using project scheduling software (such as MicroSoft Project or Primavera). Project progress can also be managed efficiently using stage gates or checkpoints [16]. This permits the manager to identify issues and challenges and

Project Name			Report Period			
Project Number			From		To	
Project Manager						
Project Status	**Planned Start Date**	**Actual Start Date**	**Date Due**	**Date Done**	**Percent complete**	**Status or Comments**
Initiating Process Tasks						
Planning Process Tasks						
Executing Process Tasks						
Monitoring and Controlling Process Tasks						
Closing Process Tasks						

FIGURE 5.4
Project status of project management processes.

deal with them early in the program. Define the baseline for the project and set the milestones toward the project completion date. The baseline plan describes the project components (such as the work breakdown structure), accompanied by a time-phased spending plan and schedule with distinct milestones that represent substantive work completion. Baselining requirements in projects provides a process for managing progress throughout the project phases. When necessary, project stage gates and baselining can indicate the need for change control. The project manager can use project status reports to monitor program progress and create consistency in communicating the work of the project to the team and management.

The issues log and risk log for the team can track decisions. The project quality management plan will include any problems with the deliverable's quality, benchmarking for the project, and quality audits.

MANAGING THE VIRTUAL TEAM

Building Team Cohesiveness Virtually

The virtual project manager is responsible for developing relationship-building strategies and activities for the team. In the collocated team, team members share the advantages of nonverbal cues, opportunities for face-to-face interactions, and social activities. Building relationships in virtual teams requires developing a social presence for team members and opportunities for team-building activities. The focus of any team-building activity should be to build trust, encourage communication, and stimulate understanding of multiple cultures within the team. Team building should be fun and provide opportunities for social interaction for the virtual team members. Team-building activities must be altered significantly to be successful in the virtual team environment. Team games can be played electronically using chat rooms or videoconferencing. Books and information on games, meeting openers, and activities using social media, smartphones, GPS, tablets, and other technology are available to help stimulate ideas for the virtual project manager [17,18]. Sharing information, bios, photos, and fun facts about team members can be done via the team Facebook page or the project website, or by including a photo and information about each team member as a pop-up with the e-mail address. One experienced virtual project manager placed a different team member "fun" information fact at the beginning of each meeting minutes. Fun information can include hobbies, favorites (TV shows, movies, food, etc.), accomplishments, fun facts, and quotes about the individual from fellow team members. Other suggestions are to have one team member share something at each team meeting or to incorporate information about the team members in team presentations. Any way that this information can be shared will work toward the goal of building the team.

Celebrating milestones and recognizing team member contributions can help a team build trust. Birthdays can be celebrated individually or collectively by month. One creative idea is for the project manager to send small gifts to team members on their birthday but ask that they open them with the team during the next conference call [19]. Gifts can also be virtual—such as e-gift cards or e-certificates. Food can also be shared virtually. A creative project manager encouraged regional teams on a rotating basis to send the other locations a box of snack foods or treats common to their culture to open and eat during the virtual teleconference meetings. "New York shipped bagels and pretzels, England sent tea and biscuits, Asia sent bento baskets, and Russia provided tea and latkes...everyone enjoyed it, and it built team spirit" [20]. A creative virtual project manager (anonymous interview) once sent her virtual team toolbags screen printed with the team's logo to celebrate that they had successfully developed a new tool for the organization, and for another project mailed candy with printed congratulatory messages to celebrate a completed milestone.

Creativity is needed to build rapport with the virtual team. The initial kick-off meeting, ideally held face-to-face and not virtually, is an excellent opportunity to begin building team cohesiveness. At this meeting, team members can be encouraged through activities to find common threads of interest and begin building relationships. Finding potential similarities can be done by sending a survey about personal interests prior to the kick-off meeting or asking questions during a conference call. When face-to-face, or if face-to-face is not possible during a videoconference, rapport can be established by matching individuals with like tastes in music, movies, use of free time, books, or hobbies. When individuals join the team after the initial kick-off, a suggestion for acculturating the new team member is to have the current team members share their bios, "fun" information, and common threads of interest with the new person electronically in "welcome" e-mails [21].

Motivating the Virtual Team

Motivation is any action or process that provides the incentive for an individual to complete a task. As Lou Holtz (former American college football coach) is quoted as saying, "Ability is what you're capable of doing. Motivation determines what you can do." The virtual manager needs to remain involved with each team member and needs to understand what motivates each one. From that information, the manager can look for motivational commonalities and develop a list of motivators that can be used for the entire team. Common motivators that tend to engage employees include the following [22]:

- Recognition
- Career development
- Relationship with manager
- Open and effective communication
- Team relationships
- Culture and shared values

Research has shown that recognition has a large impact on employee engagement. An employee's perception of recognition accounts for 56% of his or her engagement during employment [23]. In the traditional environment, recognition can range from a physical handshake and thank-you to celebrating with a lunch to providing an award or plaque for the office. In the virtual environment, however, recognition is more difficult, which is due to geographically dispersed team members. However, the fact that the team is virtual makes recognition even more important, and the remote manager needs to be actively involved and become creative in delivering recognition virtually.

Taking care that each team member is treated individually is important. An experienced project manager (anonymous interview) says to "interject human personalness into meeting and minutes" when working with virtual teams. The e-leader can keep a list of birthdays and send a note to each virtual team member on his or her birthday. Expressing appreciation for a job well done can be via a text message, e-mail, or phone call, depending upon the individual's cultural dimension and communication preference. Both positive and constructive performance feedback is an important tool for motivating employees. Respect for each individual demonstrates that the e-leader believes in each person's value and contribution to the project and is a strong motivator.

Many techniques can be used in managing virtual project teams to motivate individuals. Coaching, advising, and teaching are all motivators the e-leader can use. A successful global project manager (anonymous) says: "Diversity is inherent to the nature of virtual teams. Since different individuals have different needs for coaching and direction, and have different skills and communication styles, it is the job of the leader to recognize and build on the strengths of each team member. I have always practiced this and have found it to be very successful. I have built a team successfully from scratch, distributed globally—and have delivered very successfully on every one of my projects. The team members have thanked me for helping them grow and providing them the specific coaching they needed as individuals." Motivators can change throughout the project, and the e-leader needs to be flexible in providing incentives for the virtual team. Just as the e-leader shows flexibility in leadership styles dependent upon the situation, the e-leader shows flexibility in motivational techniques.

Types of Motivators

McCelland [24] identified three major types of motivators—affiliation, achievement, and power. A person with a high need for affiliation is motivated by positive relationships with other team members and a social environment. The individual who is motivated by achievement is concerned with success (or failure) of the assigned tasks in the project and prefers not to leave anything to chance. An individual motivated by power may need to feel some control over his or her workload and feel empowered throughout the project. In the virtual team, understanding the cultural dimension for each multicultural member can provide clues to the type of motivator(s) that may be successful for that person based upon the three types of motivators. Each cultural dimension provides a primary trait by which the virtual team member's motivational and incentive needs can be assessed. Tying McCelland's [25] motivational types to each cultural dimension provides a method by which to sync the multicultural team member to the type of incentive or activity that the e-leader can use to produce the greatest contribution for the project and achieve personal goals. Table 5.3 provides examples of how motivators can be tied to cultural dimensions for the multicultural virtual team.

TABLE 5.3

Cultural Dimensions as They Relate to Motivating Virtual Employees

Cultural Dimension	Primary Dimension Traits	McCelland's Motivational Orientation	Example Motivators
Individualistic	Self-reliant, self-sufficient	Achievement	Provide challenging tasks and autonomous work. Set goals and clear objectives and give feedback and recognition for work done well.
Collectivistic	Group orientation— family, community, company	Affiliation	Encourage team-building and relationship-building opportunities. Encourage leadership of team activities.
Low-Context	Direct, task oriented	Achievement	Give recognition as a subject matter expert. Allow opportunities to handle schedule and milestone tracking.
High-Context	Ambiguous, relationship oriented	Affiliation	Provide opportunities to acclimate and coach new team members. Allow this person to be in charge of the communications plan for the project and facilitate communications.
Low-Power Distance	Equality, no one person or group holds power	Affiliation	Give this individual the responsibility to handle the issues and risk logs and to facilitate consensus decisions and collaborative work.
High-Power Distance	Distributed power based on position or politics	Power	Provide opportunities to lead meetings and to coach and teach others on the team. Include this individual in stakeholder and sponsor meetings.
Masculine	Traditional male sex-specific roles and responsibilities	Power	Provide opportunities to lead subteams and facilitate status meetings.
Feminine	Traditional female sex-specific roles and responsibilities	Affiliation	Allow opportunities to help resolve conflict and to negotiate and problem-solve within the team.

(continued)

TABLE 5.3

Cultural Dimensions as They Relate to Motivating Virtual Employees (continued)

Cultural Dimension	Primary Dimension Traits	McCelland's Motivational Orientation	Example Motivators
Low Uncertainty Avoidance	Flexible, adapt to new ideas, take risks	Power	Recognize this individual's contributions to the team. Include this person in problem solving. Provide opportunities for collaboration and collaborative leadership.
High Uncertainty Avoidance	Avoid uncomfortable situations. Prefer familiar, structured, clear and predictable	Achievement or Affiliation	Encourage this individual to be involved with setting up team processes and procedures.

Retention

Powerful motivation increases retention. In a recent survey [26], 95% of the respondents listed "retaining talented employees" as a specific skill or trait needed to be an effective leader in the virtual environment and 94% listed "motivating others." Retaining virtual project members involves the challenge of helping the employee retain a healthy work–life balance. In the virtual environment it is easy for the team member or e-leader to become 24/7 in the project work. Creative work–life balance options are essential for the health of the employee and, ultimately, the success of the project and the organization. Eliminating some of the stressors of a virtual, global lifestyle is a good start. Some organizations provide a new suitcase when the employee has traveled a certain number of miles. Others provide vouchers good for laundry service in hotels. A progressive technology firm gives on-the-road employees sabbaticals to allow for time at home and plans face-to-face meetings at vacation spots like Disneyworld so the virtual employees' families can join them. The firm's philosophy was to retain good employees by not losing them because of family issues related to travel and, by doing so, reducing expenses needed to hire and train new people. Profit-sharing incentives and bonuses can be used as motivators to retain employees in both virtual and traditional organizations. The global workforce means that talented individuals are anywhere and everywhere, and harnessing the experience and expertise of that workforce involves skill in being able to motivate and provide meaningful incentives for project and organizational success.

Empowering the Team

The project manager who empowers the virtual team by providing assistance when needed is exhibiting the interpersonal skills of leadership, team building, motivation, influencing, decision making, political and cultural awareness, and trust building—to name a few. The successful virtual manager removes roadblocks for the team, acts as a liaison between the team and upper management, can be trusted for open communication and clear expectations, and facilitates discussion and decision making within the team [27]. The e-leader, who is a model for positive behaviors, empowers the team through encouraging independent thinking and sharing and delegating leadership. Virtual team members work autonomously and therefore often need to make decisions on their own. A project manager experienced in virtual project management (anonymous) says, "Nobody wants to work for dictator project manager. Allowing team autonomy to some extent is key to forming your remote teams." The role of the manager is to empower the team by letting the team members make decisions, solve problems, and take action through self-management. This encourages and enriches the team experience and builds trust between the manager and team member.

Empowerment can also come from within the team itself. Team members that help one another accomplish shared goals, work together effectively, and respond quickly when problems arise can produce a climate of empowerment for the team. During the planning process early in the project, the virtual team can create a group identity with a team name, logo, slogan, or brand [28]. Team branding can be a good way to establish team pride, encourage pride in the project, and empower individuals to do their best work. Allowing virtual team members to work through conflict themselves and encouraging them to respect and appreciate the contributions of the other team members can contribute to an empowered team culture. Encouraging team members, virtual or traditional, to create purpose and meaning for their work can reinforce and empower individuals to do their best work. Using assignments to increase autonomy and authority to make decisions or offering training opportunities can empower team members. Reinforcing the "team's sense of pride by periodically reminding team members how what they are doing relates to the big picture" [29] can empower individuals on the team.

Relationship Building and Trust

The complications of time, culture, and distance can greatly affect relationship building and trust on a virtual team. The project manager lays the foundation for trust in the virtual team by providing clear communications through ethical conduct and by demonstrating consistent behaviors and a positive attitude. Trust can easily be broken. Building trust and keeping it takes many behaviors, all important to be exhibited by the project manager. Figure 5.5 lists many of the behaviors that can build and keep trust on the virtual team [30].

Approaches for building trust differ across cultures. A comparison of multicultural perspectives on trust only begins to show the differences the e-leader must address in global teams. Table 5.4 details some perspectives

Behaviors That Keep Trust	Behaviors That Build Trust
Consistently keeping commitments	Clear and open communications
Sharing information	Understanding multiple cultures within the team
Acknowledging others' work	
Listening	Collaborative databases, easy access to project documentation
Acting ethically	
Being available to help	

FIGURE 5.5
Behaviors for keeping and building trust.

TABLE 5.4

Country Comparisons to Building Trust on Multicultural, Global Teams

Country	Perspectives on How to Build Trust
United States	Make deadlines, deliver on commitments, communicate candidly and clearly, act quickly and decisively, treat everyone as equals
India	Listen to explanations, encourage collaborative input, don't accept ambiguous responses as "yes" or "no" without discussion, focus on building relationships—not timelines
France	Provide the big picture and avoid details, allow time for debate, provide guidelines and processes, encourage clarity and logic, recognize chain of authority
Germany	Be punctual and efficient, allow time for conversation and explanation, provide analytical information for decision-making discussions, present items in logical order

on building trust from four countries: United States, India, France, and Germany [31]. The complexity and differences in perspectives dealing with building trust are evident in the cultural differences regarding how trust is built between individuals on teams.

There are many ways to address the topic of trust. In a team meeting, the project manager can ask the team members how trust affects the virtual work environment, and how lack of trust affects the work. Team members can be asked to list what they feel are the top three factors of trust through asynchronous technology and anonymously by poll or survey. The project manager can then relate the most common factors to the group in a synchronous meeting and encourage discussion. Individual team members can be asked to keep a "trust log" [32] to track their actions, words, and decisions relating to the trust factors. The project manager can use these logs to observe and monitor trust issues in the team. The team can periodically share their logs as part of a regular team meeting and use them to open discussion on trust issues. An example of a possible trust log is shown in Figure 5.6.

Asking newly formed virtual team members to individually list the challenges and opportunities they think they will have in the virtual environment [33] can begin a conversation that lays the foundations for relationship building and trust. This can be done with asynchronous technology. From the list provided by individual team members, the project manager can consolidate the top five to seven opportunities and challenges and then ask the team to rank them in importance. Then, bringing the team together in a synchronous meeting to discuss the top-ranking opportunities and challenges can provide an opportunity for open discussion on the concerns of the team. It can also provide the groundwork for the team's procedures, processes, and "rules" for working together.

Just as trust can be built, trust can also be broken. Table 5.5 details perspectives from four countries (United States, India, France, and Germany) on how trust can be destroyed in a virtual team [34]. The diversity in

Date	Trust Factor	Project Situation	What I Did or Said and Consequences

FIGURE 5.6
Example trust log.

TABLE 5.5

Country Comparisons to Breaking Trust on Multicultural, Global Teams

Country	Perspectives on How Trust Can Be Broken
United States	Boasting about credentials or position/power, insisting on protocol, causing work to slow without apparent reason
India	Focusing on multicultural differences and language barriers, not asking what is needed or missing for the project work to be completed, focusing on deadlines
France	Not allowing time for debate, not explaining directives and decisions, ignoring chain of authority, not acknowledging accomplishments, poor work–life balance
Germany	Rushing decisions, ignoring protocol, changing or missing deadlines, ignoring cultural and language differences, smoothing over bad news

perspectives is evident in the cultural differences regarding how trust can be broken between individuals on virtual teams.

Nonthreatening interaction can build trust and help teams overcome virtual challenges, while also emphasizing the opportunities that virtual work can offer. Placing a positive spin on the benefits of virtual project work can ultimately determine the team's attitude and ability to relate to each other. To deliver results as a virtual project manager, it is essential to understand how to develop trust in the multicultural, global team environment. Building trust is a competency that is developed over time and is not an easy competency to achieve. Building trust is hard for any team, and the challenges of virtual, multicultural team members increase this difficulty. The virtual project leader needs to set the proper tone, create opportunities for trust building, and work immediately with new teams on creative ways to build trust in the virtual environment.

Managing Social Isolation

Virtual team members may require more frequent interactions and communications to feel connected. Virtual teams can offer self-direction and autonomy but often at the price of social isolation for some team members. This is particularly true when virtual teams change members, depending upon the task or expertise needed, and then the team identity fluctuates. New team members may feel isolated, having missed any team-building activities earlier in the project. Whatever the reason, the silent virtual team member on telephone calls, the individual who does not contribute during conversations, or the one who stays in the background may be suffering from social isolation. One individual (anonymous) explained her feelings about isolation this way: "In the end, I feel that my boss never saw me as a human being because I wasn't in front of her. I think this feeds into people's fears about working virtually, that people won't work or be lazy if they are on their own, or conversely, that if you are a manager and you don't see directly what someone is doing, that they are not working. I see this as a contradiction in my company's culture—there has been tremendous support for telecommuting, and yet I don't think there has ever been support when virtual employees feel isolated or experience these types of problems."

Reasons for isolation could be multicultural issues such as language barriers, social dimensions differences, political or cross-boundary challenges, or problems with timing of meetings that are due to time zone differences. The individual may be a personality type that prefers to remain quiet and listen, think, and then analyze before speaking or hesitate to speak unless spoken to first by others. Isolation can become a serious issue in the global team. The isolated individual may have project information that others in the team need, may miss deadlines, or may have important subject matter expert information that will be vital to the success of the project. The virtual project manager should be cognizant of any individual who appears to be or become isolated during the course of the project. Despite the presence of the team's social media, website, or cyber café and good intentions of the project manager and team members, isolation can occur.

One idea for proactively discouraging the challenge of isolation is to provide minutes and handouts prior to meetings so everyone has a chance to read and understand the material prior to the meeting. Contacting the isolate prior to the meeting to ask if he or she has any questions can help bring information needed from that person forward and to the project manager's attention. There are several techniques that the e-leader can use to address isolation on the virtual team.

- Encouraging participation in meeting discussions can be accomplished by asking the isolate simple questions that require only simple answers at first, then working toward more complicated questions for better responses.
- Making sure that meetings are well facilitated and that no one person controls the conversations in the meetings is always a good guideline but can be especially helpful for the isolate to have a voice in the discussions.

- Using a round-robin technique (each person has an opportunity to speak on the topic) during conference calls is also an idea for drawing the isolate out.
- Asking the virtual team member to paraphrase what they heard and understood can draw the isolate into the conversation [35].
- Including some time during each meeting for social conversation prior to starting discussion about the project work. This may enable the isolate to get a feeling for the team and begin to join the conversation.
- Assigning a mentor or buddy for the isolate and visit with the isolate on a regular basis. One of the other team members who displays a social, amiable personality type may be a good match for this task.
- Having a regular weekly phone call to respectfully talk about the project work, any issues, and small talk can make the difference between an isolated and an engaged team member.
- Setting up a regular schedule to talk with each member of the team and keep a record of the discussions and contacts made with team members to ensure that each person on the team is receiving the same amount of attention.

An alternative solution for a hybrid team could be to allow the team member who is feeling isolated to work virtually part-time and require coming into the office the remaining time to increase the opportunity for interpersonal interaction. Also effective for hybrid team members (who may be telecommuting and periodically visit the home office) "is allocating office space for visiting virtual workers, so their identity with the home office becomes a continual physical presence in the form of an office or cubicle" [36]. Although the team member's work is tied to the virtual team, the physical presence at the home office can establish a feeling of community toward the virtual worker by those in the traditional office.

Some virtual employees may take advantage of the fact that they cannot be seen by the project manager and attempt to fade away to miss being called upon to do extra work. The project manager should be very aware of missed deadlines and deliverables, lack of communication or delayed response to e-mails or phone calls, late reports, or no response to requests—all indicators of an individual who may be "fading" from the project. Sheridan posits, "Disengaged employees are a cancer for a virtual team... an invariable lost cause, sapping and draining both time and resources" [37]. Proactive measures for this challenge include providing clear expectations early in the project and having short-term goals and deliverables so the project manager can quickly identify team members who are attempting to fade. In addition, the project manager should discuss these issues immediately with the team member, refer to the team's charter or code of conduct to enforce guidelines, encourage the team member to post working hours for everyone on the team to see, and have accountability consequences clearly indicated in the project documentation [38]. Talking to the nonworking team member may help determine any underlying issues, cultural dimensional challenges, or task allocation problems. If the problem(s) stem from lack of training, skills, or understanding technological resources, then training or coaching may resolve the issue(s).

Engaging the members of the virtual team is essential to overcoming social isolation. With only virtual relationships, some individuals can quickly begin feeling alone and unattached to the team's work. Expressions like "working in a vacuum," "feeling like the Lone Ranger," "on a deserted island," "in my own world," "castaway," and "forgotten out here" indicate lack of engagement and relationships. The virtual project manager needs to be aware of social isolates, find a way to connect them with the team, and rebuild the relationship with them.

Politics and Cyberbullying in the Virtual Environment

Just as in traditional organizations, the virtual environment is not without its share of political issues. Honest and clear communication and expectations can limit political issues in the virtual team. The virtual project manager should recognize the warning signs of political issues, such as e-mails from subteams within the project using the terms *we* and *them* to explain issues. If team members appear to become competitive and limit communication to other team members or individuals, the project manager should refocus on teamwork and provide activities that encourage working as a team. This can occur with individual competitiveness and between cross-functional teams. Personal agendas can also become an issue, even on the virtual team. Again, the e-leader should focus on team development and also emphasize team successes over individual successes. Respect can become a political challenge, especially with multicultural teams, and the e-leader should work with the team on understanding multicultural differences.

The virtual project manager should pay particular attention to any carbon copies (cc's) on e-mails and to group e-mail lists. The development of cliques in virtual teams is just as possible as it is in the traditional collocated team. Watch for individuals who are regularly left out of the discussions and for individuals who seem to interact with just a certain few team members. Some of this can be due to the type of work being done for the project, but it can also be an indication of cliques and raise potential isolate problems. Drawing a sociogram of the team's virtual communications can be helpful. A sociogram can help analyze choices or preferences within a group by mapping the communication patterns seen in the group and connecting the individuals to the other individuals on the team who are communicating with each other. The resulting diagram quickly shows those with few or no communication links. Figure 5.7 shows an example of a sociogram.

Cliques can be identified as groups of three or more people within a larger group who all choose to communicate with each other but not with anyone else. Figure 5.7 shows A, B, and C as a possible clique on the team. Isolates are identified by individuals who have no connections to the others in the group. Figure 5.7 shows D as an isolate on the team. The sociogram can plot the structure of interpersonal relations in the team and provide insight for the virtual project manager who cannot physically see the dynamics of the virtual team members or how they communicate with each other. When communication cliques appear on the team that isolate individuals who should be part of the communications flow, the virtual manager must quickly respond by refocusing the team. A face-to-face meeting, virtual or not virtual, can effectively refocus the team on the importance of inclusive communications. A review of the communications plan, team charter, and code of conduct can also refocus the team on the importance of open communications. Reviewing and updating the project mailing lists, newsgroup

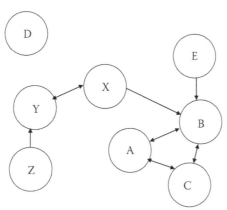

FIGURE 5.7
Sociogram.

lists, and contact lists can prevent communication cliques from appearing on the virtual team. As a hybrid virtual project manager, avoid any temptation to rely on team members on-site more than the virtual team members. Often dependence upon collocated team members can evolve into cliques that exclude the virtual team members.

Cyberbullying refers to the electronic posting of messages that are intended to harm or embarrass the receiver. These messages are hostile, deliberate, and frequently repeated and include communications that intimidate, manipulate, or discredit the recipient. These messages can be sent by one individual or several individuals to the victim. Because cyberbullying is a relatively new act, laws have been implemented in some areas and are currently being addressed by legislation. A problem commonly associated with children and adolescents, cyberbullying can also take place between adults in the work environment. Statistics from the Waitt Institute for Violence Prevention indicate that one in three employees has personally experienced some type of workplace bullying [39]. Examples of cyberbullying are communications that are malicious or threatening; feature offensive content about ethnicity, religion, or sexual preference; publicly shame or demean the recipient; or include manipulated messages or images of the individual.

e-Leaders should be aware that cyberbullying often goes unreported. Victims may show signs of low self-esteem and low morale or seem angry or depressed. Victims may avoid team interactions and activities, including meetings. To discourage cyberbullying, e-leaders and organizations should promote a workplace where it is not allowed, have a policy against cyberbullying that also details the consequences if someone does it, and provide training and examples of cyberbullying if necessary. The virtual team's code of conduct should address cyberbullying as an action that will not be tolerated in the virtual environment. Any indications of cyberbullying in the virtual team should be brought to the attention of the executive managers and proper authorities.

Indicators of Inappropriate Virtual Team Member "Fit"

Not every personality is adaptable to working on virtual project teams. Certain competencies in individuals will provide the framework for success in global, multicultural teams. Performance reviews, discussions with functional managers, discussions with peer team members, and interviewing potential virtual team members can be ways to identify the competencies needed for that individual to be successful in the virtual environment.

Competencies to look for include (1) willingness to take accountability, (2) excellent interpersonal skills, (3) technological competence, (4) ability to work independently, and (5) ability to work well with a team [40]. In addition, the virtual project team member needs to be able to handle limited social interaction, have good organizational and time management skills, communicate effectively, be self-motivated, and be able to focus on tasks to completion [41]. Not everyone is self-disciplined enough to be able to work effectively in an unstructured environment and autonomously. Working remotely does not mean that company procedures do not apply. Time tracking, personal time usage, vacation time usage, and expense reports apply to the virtual employee just as they do to the traditional employee.

The virtual project manager needs to understand the competencies required for successful virtual work. If a team member is struggling, it is the responsibility of the project manager to deal with the situation, just as the traditional project manager has to deal with the situation. Examples of poor virtual fits in one project team (anonymous interview) include:

- a team member who was controlling, direct, and not political in his dealings with the other team members and was released after coaching was not successful
- a virtual team member who felt that travel for the team was his chance to party on the road was dismissed after getting arrested for driving under the influence
- a lead technical worker let go due to poor communication skills, inability to deal with change, and impatience with the other virtual team members
- a virtual worker was asked to leave because she was never available, didn't produce results, and couldn't (or wouldn't) manage her time

Just as some students are unable to study and learn in a virtual classroom, some individuals are unable to function and work in a virtual project environment.

E-ETHICS

Ethical behavior by leaders in organizations is important in traditional and virtual environments. Developing ethical management skills is essential for project managers because the project manager often has to deal with rapid change and uncertainty—key factors that lead to moral decision making [42]. A competent project manager, as described by the Project Management Institute [43], should be able to demonstrate defined and accepted standards of personal behavior and be able to apply them to project activities. Project management competencies include ethical behavior "governed by responsibility, respect, fairness and honesty" [44]. Project work tends to be high profile and be highly visible in many organizations, causing pressure and stress on the project team to do whatever is necessary to make the project succeed. Ethical behavior is often the first thing compromised in a high-risk environment [45].

Virtual team members often lack immediate feedback because of location and can be left on their own to make critical decisions. When ethical issues are at stake, the asynchronous nature of virtual team communications adds the benefit of being able to think through a response prior to submission. This allows the opportunity to review the response with fresh eyes, less emotional attachment, and thus increased objectivity. The virtual team environment may be more conducive to adhering to an objective professional and ethical standard because of the nature of working virtually. The virtual team member may make better decisions in a virtual environment, where there is less peer pressure. Conversely, as can be evidenced by story after story in the press, the virtual environment can lead to anonymity that provides some individuals the opportunity to behave in ways that they never would in a traditional work environment. The lack of face-to-face responsibility and accountability can compromise some individuals' integrity. Without the other members of a team physically present, a team member's decision could possibly be compromised by the fact that "no one would notice" if unethical actions were taken. A formal chain of command should be in place even when time zones are 24/7 so that team members are never left to question what the expected response should be or to whom they can refer for guidance. Establishing a code of conduct up front, together with a work breakdown structure, a communications plan, and a team or project charter all work in concert to lay the foundation for ethical project work.

Unethical use of sensitive material is listed as a major issue for e-leaders [46]. Software programs are available to overtly monitor electronic messages and inform the sender of the ethical implications of the message while also providing corrective instructions. The downside of these programs is that they may cause reliance upon the messages and lead to a lack of moral decision making by the employee. They can also be perceived by the employees as a lack of trust by the project manager. Computer use cannot be managed by the virtual e-leader. Ethical decisions related to computer use are influenced by the individual's own personal ethics first, then by any informal ethical code in the organization, and then by the organization's formal code of ethics [47]. By clearly identifying the roles and responsibilities of each team member, the e-leader can assist the virtual team in understanding their roles and the conduct considered appropriate for the team.

In addition, virtual communications can create a tendency for more aggressive and disrespectful behavior because the lack of face-to-face interactions can encourage behaviors that otherwise might not be acceptable [43]. However, these behaviors can also cause the sender to be countered with similar behavior, which inhibits most virtual communicators from volleying emotionally irresponsible and unethical virtual communications.

"By realizing how ethics differ in virtual teams from traditional face-to-face teams, individuals managing virtual teams will be able to provide positive, ethical leadership to virtual project teams, resulting in the leadership skills to discern moral dilemmas, prioritize values, assess risks, protect privacy, and make ethical decisions" [48]. The project manager is responsible for monitoring for unethical behavior, responding quickly to unethical behaviors should they arise, and guiding the team back toward a caring, trusting environment.

Case Study 5.1: From Challenged to Achieving

[As told to the author by "Antonio," a virtual project manager from a large U.S.-based organization (anonymous interview)]

OVERVIEW

I was a project manager and I was assigned to work with a development team to meet the reporting needs of certain departments. I actually worked in San Diego and my team was in Southern California, outside of Los Angeles. I knew that the person I was replacing had left and that things had just not gone well for everybody. I had some information about the business requirements, but the team had already provided a mid-level requirements document.

The first thing I did when I got the project was to have a meeting and we introduced ourselves. I felt it was more important for us to get to know each other. It wasn't face-to-face because there was no budget for me to travel. So I set up a conference call to introduce myself, and we just chatted so I could figure out who was talking and who was not talking, who was being the leader—like you do when you have a stakeholders meeting, you just size the situation up, who you are going to have difficulty with, and that kind of stuff. So we just talked about what they wanted, what was working for them, and what wasn't working for them. And they were just basically saying, "Just leave us alone and all we want to do is code." Very typical, right? I knew who was talking and who wasn't talking and could tell who thought this was stupid. I made a list of their concerns, asked some questions, and then I just left it at that.

They mentioned some problems they had had. Then I said, "Based on the limited information that I have, when we come up to the next business requirement request for this new report, what can I do to make sure we don't fall into the same pitfalls like the first request right off the bat?" I spent about 30–45 minutes talking with them about what was working and what wasn't working because I did not want to hit those same potholes the first time through.

So then it came time for our twice-weekly meeting to talk about what's new, what they're struggling with, what issues they have, what they are working on, how are things going—it was just a development piece, so it was a lot like an agile process. We would get the requests in and we'd deliver in a week or two, and then we'd give them directly to the business and the business was the one who would then figure out if they would work. So we got our first request in and I said we could maybe avoid some of the potholes that they had had in the past. So we discussed it and talked about it, and they said they could just add the request on to another report. I asked if this was what everyone believed, and someone piped up and said, "You know, because they want this and this and this with the report—data elements—that it might be easier, instead of using this report, to use a different report so then we're not having to remove things and we could build a little bit more." So I began to understand how they were thinking and what the processes were. They all agreed and they were done with the request in about three days! And they said it would take about five. And so we turned it over to the business and the business said, "Yes, this is great," and they had no issues and no concerns. So I knew I was dealing with a very high performing team. They had done what their customers had asked for, in the format that the customer wanted, and I had asked those questions about being sure that they weren't falling into the same potholes again. There were a couple of projects that were still in flight and had not been done, and this was Tuesday, and I think they were done by Friday. So when we met again, they asked for more work. So I asked, "What are some of the other issues you have had in the past?" and we put our heads together again. Because I had taken the time to meet with them, even though they had kind of thought it was a waste of time, we really developed a working relationship. My takeaway from it was that they began to have the faith in me, and I had given them a leg up so they weren't as frustrated trying to deliver the reports. Within three months the team was underutilized, we had streamlined the process so much, and they weren't having to do all the rework.

So in the beginning, for me, inheriting an existing team when you're all offsite—it was really all about how I insert myself into the team and fill that space and build trust. Because I really believe that in virtual teams you have to have trust in the individuals and especially whoever is leading the team. When you're dealing with people offsite, you have to take them at their word—it's not like you can see them and whether they're working or not working—you're really limited. It's not like you can check in with somebody here or in the next building—you have to develop a culture of trust and openness to set up a high-performance team.

DEBRIEF

Antonio recognizes that coming into a team that had leadership challenges and was already through the midlevel requirements documentation requires special leadership competencies. Antonio realizes that the team has a negative attitude toward leadership. They tell him, "Just leave us alone and all we want to do is code."

His first action is to attempt to build trust with the team: "The first thing I did when I got the project was to have a meeting and we introduced ourselves. I felt it was more important for us to get to know each other." The best way for this type of meeting is face-to-face; however, Antonio was not able to do a face-to-face meeting. Instead he opts for a conference call to introduce himself. A better option would have been some type of videoconferencing, so the new team could put a face with his voice, and Antonio could actually see the team. Instead, Antonio chooses a conference call and listens carefully to the team's interpersonal interactions and communications, drawing a sociogram of the discourse in his mind. He says, "We just chatted so I could figure out who was talking and who was not talking, who was being the leader—like you do when you have a stakeholders meeting, you just size the situation up, who you are going to have difficulty with and that kind of stuff," and, "I knew who was talking and who wasn't talking and could tell who thought this was stupid."

To build trust he intends to show that he will be a positive leader for the team, so Antonio asks the team what they need—"what was working for them and what wasn't working for them." He says, "I made a list of their concerns, asked some questions," and, "what can I do to make sure we don't fall into the same pitfalls." By saying this he shows empathy with the team's challenges and, if he follows through by actually helping the team, can build the trust he needs to make the team and project successful. At the next meeting, he does follow through with his commitment to help: "So we got our first request in and I said we could maybe avoid some of the potholes that they had had in the past. So we discussed it and talked about it and they said they could just add the request on to another report." Notice that as the leader he does not tell them what to do, but he guides them into a discussion about some ideas of how to improve the process. Then he asks for affirmation and confirmation of the new ideas: "I asked if this was what everyone believed." At this point, Antonio finds that his efforts at building trust with this team are beginning to pay off. Not in consensus to his ideas, but in the team feeling free to debate ideas and discuss options with him present. He says that "someone piped up and said, 'You know, because they want this and this and this with the report—data elements—that it might be easier, instead of using this report, to use a different report so then we're not having to remove things and we could build a little bit more.'" This was a major breakthrough for Antonio as the virtual project manager and for the virtual project team. He exclaims, "They all agreed and they were done with the request in about three days!"

The team begins to see improvement in the work process, and their trust in Antonio grows. At the next meeting, the team asks for more work, but Antonio slows them down and probes further into the processes that have held this obviously capable team back. He says, "So when we met again, they asked for more work. So I said, 'What are some of the other issues you have had in the past?' and we put our heads together again." By doing this, he empowers the virtual team by exhibiting the interpersonal skills of leadership, team building, influencing, and trust building. He successfully uses open communication and clear expectations to facilitate a discussion and encourage more independent thinking and idea sharing. The team responds, and Antonio says, "They began to have the faith in me, and I had given them a leg up so they weren't as frustrated trying to deliver the reports," and he reports that the team's productivity takes a remarkable turn upward. He concludes by saying, "You have to develop a culture of trust and openness to set up a high-performance team."

Case Study 5.2: Same Country—Different Worlds

[As told to the author by "Mona," an employee of a global financial organization (anonymous interview)]

SCENARIO

I worked for an independent investment firm recently acquired by a large bank in Chicago, on a project to consolidate systems for the two institutions. The investment firm was accustomed to working virtually, as the company had been evenly split between New Jersey and Sacramento—plus, the many people in Sacramento had to be used to working virtually with the stock market, including working East Coast hours. Plus, the system that processed the company's trades was run by a vendor out of New Jersey.

There were two major areas of disconnect between our investment firm and the bank taking it over:

- One was that the bank was used to doing all their business in person and accustomed to everyone doing business with them to travel to their company headquarters.
- Second, their project managers had been trained to come into a company to dismantle—but in this case, the bank had bought the investment firm because it was acquiring a function that it didn't have—stock trading. However, the bank project team kept

behaving as if they were in a take-over situation. They didn't know how to work to integrate functions or to include the other teams in decision making.

For instance, for one particular subproject team I was on, when we would have calls with people in Sacramento in one conference room and with people in Chicago in the other, it would be very hard for the Sacramento team to follow. People in Chicago did not talk directly to the people on the phone, but would chat in the room with each other. There was no way for the West Coast team to follow the side discussions. They also kept leaving out the Sacramento manager, and kept "forgetting" that his product and systems weren't being eliminated but were being incorporated into the bank. I remember a Chicago team member making reference to when the mainframe system was being retired—which it wasn't, as that was the platform we were migrating to.

Most appalling to me, there was one incident in which the Chicago team was discussing a major decision that had been made for the project. The Sacramento manager expressed surprise, as he had not been aware of a decision. The Chicago folks answered that it had been made the week before, and he had been absent. Of course, at that point, the Sacramento manager completely lost his temper, as he was forced to explain to them that he was a key stakeholder and that he was a necessary decision maker.

DEBRIEF QUESTIONS

1. What communications issues do you see in this scenario? Explain how a team charter could help this team.
2. What cultural issues do you see in this scenario? How are the West Coast and Chicago teams culturally different? Give examples of what the project manager could do to blend the two cultures.
3. Are the vision and project overview statement for the project clearly understood by the project team? How can the project manager help this team understand the shared goal(s) for this project?
4. Why do you think communications broke down and the Sacramento manager was left out of an important decision? Who should be responsible for the agenda and minutes for a virtual project? Is there more to this conflict than just missing a meeting or not getting the meeting minutes?

Case Study 5.3: Out of Her Sight—Out of a Job

[As told to the author by "Margot," a virtual project manager from an international organization (anonymous interview)]

OVERVIEW

In 2011, after a big reorganization, my old division was dismantled and I ended up telecommuting for a new division with a new manager based in Montreal, Canada. My new manager and I talked about my visiting Montreal, but she ended up with unexpected surgery that took her out of the office for several months.

So, here I was, new to the department, though not new to the company or to virtual project management, so I did the best I could. I was told that the project I was assigned was in "red" status. It also had an MRIA (matter requiring immediate attention) as one of its deliverables, due in only two months. I hit the ground running and did what I thought was an excellent job of coordinating the project, keeping things moving, and meeting required dates. As I was doing this, I didn't have much guidance, as the manager above me was very senior and didn't have time to spend with me.

Imagine my shock when my manager came back and she used the opportunity to go on a "fishing expedition" against me. There was a technical lead on the project who I had been warned was a troublemaker, and I suspect he egged her on. I got a surprise phone call from my manager in which she told me that she had talked to many stakeholders who said bad things about my work and that she didn't believe that I had done anything in her absence. From then on, it was downhill. She took me off the project, and then said she was going to reassign me to something else, but didn't "find a place for me." I ended up with a negative performance review, which I had *never* had in all my years of work, and ended up on the layoff list. In a way, the layoff a short time later was a relief.

DEBRIEF

This case study highlights two serious issues: (1) isolation and (2) relationship building and politics in the virtual environment.

ISOLATION

Margot feels very isolated in her new position. There was no opportunity for her to meet her new manager face-to-face when she began the job, and this began a spiral of loneliness and isolation. Her new boss is out of the office ("She ended up with unexpected surgery that took her out of the office for several months"), and Margot has no relationship with her senior management ("The manager above me was very senior and didn't have time to spend with me"). Even virtual project managers need frequent interactions and communications with their management to feel connected and avoid social peer isolation. Sending get-well cards, telephone calls, and visits (not work related) to her new manager may have helped build their relationship during this estrangement. Margot's situation was exasperated by the change to a new division with new management ("So, here I was, new to the department"). It is not unusual for new team members at any level to feel isolated, especially in Margot's situation where there was no opportunity for team- or relationship-building activities at the time of her transfer. Compounding the issue are the political or cross-boundary changes Margot made at her management level when she took the new job. Assigned to a difficult project already in trouble, Margot soldiered on alone until isolation issues caught up with her.

RELATIONSHIP BUILDING AND POLITICS IN THE VIRTUAL ENVIRONMENT

Margot's virtual position was not without political issues. She became overwhelmed with the project, managing the documentation and details while letting relationships and politics take second place: "I hit the ground running, and did what I thought was an excellent job of coordinating the project, keeping things moving, and meeting required dates." As the project manager, she did not attempt to build a relationship with the technical worker on her team who she knew could become a problem. She admits, "There was a technical lead on the project who I had been warned was a troublemaker, and I suspect he egged her on." Her relationship with this individual should have been a priority as soon as she found out about the potential political challenge he presented to the project and herself. Team members that appear competitive and limit communication should be refocused on teamwork and provided activities that encourage teamwork. This is particularly true in cross-functional teams when individuals (such as the technical lead) may have a personal agenda. Margot also forgot the importance of relationship building with one of the most political of all project groups—stakeholders. This is evident by her saying, "I got a surprise phone call from my manager in which she told me that she had talked to many stakeholders." If open communication and good relationships with stakeholders were evident, then someone surely would have notified her of the manager's "fishing expedition"—provided that what the manager was telling her was true. She also says, "imagine my shock," an indication that even after her manager returned, Margot had not built a relationship with her. Margot's all-consuming focus on doing the best she could, hitting the ground running, coordinating the project, keeping things moving, and meeting required dates caused her to fail to notice the politics around her affecting her relationships. Compounded with her isolation issues, the resulting end to her career with the company was not a surprise. She says, "In a way, the layoff a short time later was a relief."

NOTES

Anonymous quotes from virtual project managers are taken from survey responses in:

Lee, M. R. (2011). *e-Leadership for project managers: A study of situational leadership and virtual project success.* ProQuest, UMI Dissertation Publishing.

Anonymous interviews:

Lee, M. R. (2013). *Interview by M. R. Lee* [Tape recording.] Springfield, IL.

REFERENCES

1. Martin, A., & Bal, V. (2007). *The state of teams.* (CCL Research White Paper). Center for Creative Leadership (CCL). Retrieved from www.cci.org.
2. Project Management Institute. (2013). *A guide to the project management body of knowledge: PMBOK guide* (5th ed.). Newton Square, PA: Project Management Institute.
3. Duarte, D., & Snyder, N. (1999). *Mastering virtual teams.* San Francisco: Jossey-Bass.
4. Pauleen, D. (2004). *Virtual teams: Projects, protocol and processes* (p. 260). Hershey, PA: Idea Group, Inc.
5. Fisher, K., & Fisher, M. (2011). *Manager's guide to virtual teams.* New York: McGraw-Hill.
6. Duarte, D., & Snyder, N. (1999). *Mastering virtual teams.* San Francisco: Jossey-Bass.
7. Fisher, K., & Fisher, M. (2011). *Manager's guide to virtual teams.* New York: McGraw-Hill.
8. Fisher, K., & Fisher, M. (2011). *Manager's guide to virtual teams.* New York: McGraw-Hill.
9. Wysocki, R. K. (2009). *Effective project management: Traditional, agile, extreme* (5th ed.). New York: Wiley.

10. Lee, M. R. (2009). E-ethical leadership for virtual project teams. *International Journal of Project Management, 27*(5), 456–463. doi:10.1016/j.ijproman.2008.05.012.
11. Software Engineering Institute. (2001). *People capability maturity model* (Version 2). Carnegie Mellon University. Retrieved from http://www.sei.cmu.edu/pub/documents/01.reports/pdf/01mm001.pdf.
12. Project Management Institute. (n.d.). *PMI code of ethics and professional conduct.* Retrieved from http://www.pmi.org/codeofethicsPDF.
13. Project Management Institute. (2013). *A guide to the project management body of knowledge: PMBOK guide* (5th ed.) (p. 1). Newton Square, PA: Project Management Institute.
14. Garton, C., & Wegryn, K. (2006). *Managing without walls.* Lewisville, TX: Mc Press Online, LP.
15. Zofi, Y. S. (2011). *A manager's guide to virtual teams.* New York: AMACOM.
16. Brown, J. T. (2008). *The handbook of program management* (8th ed.). New York: McGraw-Hill.
17. Chen, J. (2012). *50 digital team building games: Fast, fun meeting openers, group activities, and adventures using social media, smart phones, GPS, tablets, and more.* New York: Wiley and Sons.
18. Scannell, M., Abrams, M., & Mulvihill, M. (2011). *Big book of virtual teambuilding games: Quick, effective activities to build communication, trust and collaboration from anywhere!* New York: McGraw-Hill.
19. Zofi, Y. S. (2011). *A manager's guide to virtual teams.* New York: AMACOM.
20. Zofi, Y. S. (2011). *A manager's guide to virtual teams* (p. 51). New York: AMACOM.
21. Zofi, Y. S. (2011). *A manager's guide to virtual teams.* New York: AMACOM.
22. Sheridan, K. (2012). *The virtual manager.* Pompton Plains, NJ: Career Press.
23. Sheridan, K. (2012). *The virtual manager.* Pompton Plains, NJ: Career Press.
24. McCelland, D. (1961). *The achieving society.* New York: Free Press.
25. McCelland, D. (1961). *The achieving society.* New York: Free Press.
26. Pulley, M. L., Sessa, V. I., Fleenor, J., & Pohlmann, T. (2001). e-Leadership: Separating the reality from the hype. *Leadership in Action—LIA, 21*(4), 3–6.
27. Brown, J. T. (2008). *The handbook of program management* (8th ed.). New York: McGraw-Hill.
28. DeRosa, D. M., & Lepsinger, R. (2010). *Virtual team success: A practical guide for working and leading from a distance.* San Francisco: Jossey-Bass.
29. DeRosa, D. M., & Lepsinger, R. (2010). *Virtual team success: A practical guide for working and leading from a distance* (p. 74). San Francisco: Jossey-Bass.
30. Zofi, Y. S. (2011). *A manager's guide to virtual teams.* New York: AMACOM.
31. Settle-Murphy, N. (2013). Building trust calls for different approaches across different cultures. *Guided Insights.* Boxborough, MA. Retrieved from http://www.guidedinsights.com/newsletter_detail.asp?PageID = 11488.
32. Duarte, D., & Snyder, N. (1999). *Mastering virtual teams.* San Francisco: Jossey-Bass.
33. Zofi, Y. S. (2011). *A manager's guide to virtual teams.* New York: AMACOM.
34. Settle-Murphy, N. (2013). Building trust calls for different approaches across different cultures. *Guided Insights.* Boxborough, MA. Retrieved from http://www.guidedinsights.com/newsletter_detail.asp?PageID = 11488.
35. Zofi, Y. S. (2011). *A manager's guide to virtual teams.* New York: AMACOM.
36. Lee, M. R. (2009). E-ethical leadership for virtual project teams. *International Journal of Project Management, 27*(5), 456–463 (p. 461). doi:10.1016/j.ijproman.2008.05.012.
37. Sheridan, K. (2012). *The virtual manager.* Pompton Plains, NJ: Career Press.
38. Zofi, Y. S. (2011). *A manager's guide to virtual teams.* New York: AMACOM.

39. CQR. (2007). Workplace cyberbullying. *Media Links 2007 Whitepapers.* Retrieved from http://www.cqrconsulting.com/disconnect/whitepapers/115-workplace- cyber-bullying/default.htm.

40. Fisher, K., & Fisher, M. (2011). *Manager's guide to virtual teams.* New York: McGraw-Hill.

41. Goncalves, M. (2005). *Managing virtual projects.* New York: McGraw-Hill.

42. Pinto, J., Thoms, P., Trailer, J., Palmer, T., & Govekar, M. (1998). *Project leadership from theory to practice.* Newtown Square, PA: Project Management Institute.

43. Cranford, M. (1996). The social trajectory of virtual reality: Substantive ethics in a world without constraints. *Technology in Society, 18*(1), 79–92.

44. Project Management Institute. (2007). *Project manager competency development (PMCD) framework* (2nd ed.). Newton Square, PA: Project Management Institute.

45. Pinto, J., Thoms, P., Trailer, J., Palmer, T., & Govekar, M. (1998). *Project leadership from theory to practice.* Newtown Square, PA: Project Management Institute.

46. Ariss, S., Nykodym, N., & Cole-Laramore, A. A. (2002). Trust and technology in the virtual organization. *S.A.M. Advanced Management Journal, 67*(4), 22–25.

47. Pierce, M. A., & Henry, J. W. (1996). Computer ethics: The role of personal, informal, and formal codes. *Journal of Business Ethics, 15*(4), 425–427.

48. Lee, M. R. (2009). E-ethical leadership for virtual project teams. *International Journal of Project Management, 27*(5), 456–463. doi:10.1016/j.ijproman.2008.05.012.

Index